Praise for *Collateral Ha|*

Wow! I saw great success within the VERY FIRST WEEK of following her guidance. Not only do I highly recommend Christine, I encourage everyone to read her book as soon as possible as your life will change in the most positive ways, and you will quickly see success.

Julie Brown

This is not self-help; but is self-creation. Christine Waldner provides an immeasurable amount of inspiration and motivation. She has quickly become one of the most inspirational and influential people in my life.

Derek Cruickshank

Collateral Happiness
The Power Behind The Facade

A comprehensive, step-by-step guide to meeting
the most significant human in your life—you.

CHRISTINE WALDNER, BBA, Life Coach

Copyright © 2018 by Christine Waldner
ISBN 978-1-7751847-0-6

All Rights Reserved. No parts of this book may be reproduced or transmitted in any form without permission in writing from the author, except by a reviewer who may quote for review purposes. For more information, please email the publisher at:

info@christinewaldner.com

www.christinewaldner.com
Calgary, Alberta

Edited by Marie Beswick-Arthur, www.mariebeswickarthur.com
Cover photo by Howard's Cove Photography
Cover Design by the author
Book Design by Dominique Petersen, www.AuthorConsultants.org

Published in CANADA
Rendlaw Publishing

The author speaks from her perspective and experience. The author disclaims any liability, loss, or risk incurred by individuals who act on the information contained herein. The author believes the advice presented here is sound, but readers cannot hold Christine Waldner or Rendlaw Publishing responsible for either the actions they take or the results of those actions.

The dynamic nature of the internet dictates that web addresses or links herein contained may change after publication.

To every person who struggles
to find happiness and purpose in life.

Acknowledgements

Thank you to everyone who made my research and this book possible. Without you, there would be no book. There would be no realization of *Collateral Happiness* in my own life.

Scott, Ayden, and Ainsley: my deepest thanks and love for all your support, patience, encouragement, and enthusiasm to stand by me. You gave me the courage and 'will' to continue, to never give up despite the numerous times I wanted to. You believed in me more than I believed in myself, balanced giving me space and attention, and loved me even during my worst of times, accepting me as me. You helped me realize that I too could learn to love myself as you love me. As said by Richard Bach,

> *A soulmate is someone who has locks that fit our keys, and keys to fit our locks. When we feel safe enough to open the locks, our truest selves step out and we can be completely and honestly who we are; we can be loved for who we are and not for who we're pretending to be.*

I am forever grateful for your love, Scott, which was powerful enough for me to do the work of self-discovery, of awakening.

Sam Lee, my first client: through the years you allowed me to practice and learn with you and through you. You gave me more encouragement than I ever gave myself, always praised me, and accepted me for me—I am eternally grateful.

To my editor, Marie Beswick-Arthur, who quickly became my soul-sister. You've encouraged, supported, and challenged me to put my best work forward; never shutting me down during the brainstorming process, always keeping me on task, and providing me the structure required to formulate this book. I laugh, thinking of the very first manuscript I ever sent you, and how it beautifully transformed into what it is today because of your dedication, and that of Richard Beswick-Arthur: thank you.

I would like to express my sincere gratitude to Dominique Petersen, of New Author Publishing Services, who helped me prepare this book for print. Her patience, dedication, expertise, and care for quality went above and beyond anything I could have hoped for. Thank you so much for helping me to complete this book. You taught me a great deal.

Andrea Thatcher, you helped me connect to the outside world. You allowed me to grow big, accepted me and my big dreams, and helped me to stop hiding from who I really was. You filled in many blanks I required to fully unleash my inner-warrior, such as the need for commitment, discomfort, and learning: such deep appreciation for your talents and your friendship.

I am thankful to every friend, family member, client, acquaintance, and colleague. Every interaction revealed a lesson, encouragement, or support that helped me uncover seeds of my soul and made my journey possible.

Lastly, I honour the work of Tony Robbins, Oprah Winfrey, Dan Millman, and Vicktor Frankl. Each has deeply inspired me and my work.

Table of Contents

Introduction

PART I
ENCOURAGEMENT

Dear Reader.. 3
The Monologues of the Lower Self....................... 5
The List.. 9
Let's Pause 11
Inspiration About Success.............................. 12

PART II
FOUNDATIONAL UNDERSTANDING OF COLLATERAL HAPPINESS

STEP ONE: The Basic Science of the Body 21
STEP TWO: The Basic Emotions of the Mind 36
THIS IS JANE.. 54
The Approach and Formula for the Creation of
 Collateral Happiness.................................. 64
STEP THREE: The Basics on the Laws of Spirit (Human Nature). 69

PART III
HABITS OF COLLATERAL HAPPINESS

STEP FOUR: Appreciating the Habits..................... 79
Habit #1: Movement..................................... 85
Habit #2: Nutrition 94
EAT JANE, EAT.. 100
Habit #3: Spiritual Practice 106

Habit #4: Creativity/Learning 114
Habit #5: Positive Relationships 120
Habit #6: Mindfulness. 126
THINK JANE, THINK. 135

PART IV
GETTING TO KNOW YOU:
THE SELF-AWARENESS OF COLLATERAL HAPPINESS

STEP FIVE: Becoming Self-Aware 145
Awareness #1: Goals and Commitments 146
Awareness #2: Passion and Purpose. 154
Awareness #3: Identifying Core Values 161
Awareness #4: Scheduling and Prioritizing 166
Awareness #5: Self-Limiting Beliefs 169
DEEP JANE, DEEP. 172
Awareness #6: Pain and Pleasure 177
Awareness #7: Metaprograms 179
Awareness #8: Changing Our Language 183
Awareness #9: Power of Positive Influence. 184
LISTEN JANE, LISTEN 190

PART V
ROMANCING THE SELF:
LOVE AND AUTHENTICITY OF COLLATERAL HAPPINESS

STEP SIX: A Primer on Self Love 205
Self-Love #1: Six Core Human Needs 206
OWN IT JANE, OWN IT 209
Self-Love #2: Forgiveness and Acceptance of Self 213
GOODBYE (old) JANE, GOODBYE 225
STEP SEVEN: Revealing Our Authentic Self 229
Authenticity #1: Stepping Outside Our Comfort Zone. 231
Authenticity #2: Facing Our Fears 241
RAW JANE, RAW 246

PART VI
SOUL SHIFT OF COLLATERAL HAPPINESS

Experiencing Collateral Happiness........................251
Side Effects of Transformation..........................256
ROAR JANE, ROAR 257
On the Fear of Our Own Ego............................259
The Afterlogue of the Higher Self........................262

About the Author

Introduction

When we truly listen to happy and successful people speak, or read their books, we recognize that they have put in the work. Most will have quite a history.

It took me many years, but I eventually learned the greatest lesson of all:

**The only difference between wanting to be a happy person and being a happy person is 'doing the work'.
We are defined by our actions, not our thoughts.
We must do the work. It is not enough to think about it.**

Since I've only lived in my shoes, I cannot assume how another individual feels; the examples in this book are abstracts of myself as a learner, grower, and coach.

My work has been about happiness, and the result is that is has helped me create my own. I truly wish that these lessons will do the same for you.

In a perfect world, every person would go through a full 'practical' program of learning how to create happiness. If happiness is the ultimate goal, then we need a course that echoes practical application similar to driving lessons, learning a new language, or first aid.

It is my intention to begin teaching a program to learn how to obtain inner-happiness.

Whether we take credit or non-credit courses, all require work. There are no free passes, neither are participation ribbons distributed freely; the curriculum provided here in *Collateral Happiness* requires diligent, ongoing work. Graduation will follow, its rewards life-enhancing—delivering so much more than a certificate ever could.

We are creatures of habit. We try to beat the system and skip steps. We pay thousands of dollars to people who take advantage of our inability to commit to the work of creating happiness; shortcut vendors.

We convince ourselves that people who are happy, and experience success, are just lucky, and are the chosen few. The thing is: those people worked diligently to define and customize personal success, based on inner-happiness, and then created it.

Ten years of soul searching led me to a place to have the courage and patience to write this book. My need to liberate my own soul initiated the journey, and my discoveries led me to a purpose: to share these findings with others who struggle to create happiness and find purpose in life.

Feeling horribly inadequate in myriad areas, I surrendered to experience growth, and collect the seeds of innovation. I discovered the difference between inner-happiness and artificial happiness, and the powerful role of the former to completely change lives.

And the earth shifted under my feet.

The research may have been the catalyst to change, but work beyond listening, reciting, and appreciating a concept was required.

PART I
ENCOURAGEMENT

Dear Reader

Before you read this book, I invite you to hold it close to your heart and introduce yourself as you would to someone you intuitively feel will be a lifelong confidante.

If you like, stretch your imagination to visualize that the knowledge imparted in this book—delivered to you in steps—will inform your values and become an integral part of you.

The main thing is, get personal. Form a relationship with this guide; for she will reveal a path for which you have long been prepared, and offer you the role of a lifetime.

Consider picking up a scribbler or journal to accompany your journey through *Collateral Happiness,* to collateral happiness; one in which you can note-take from the voice in your head as you sort through your thoughts and feelings. You might find it helpful to rewrite questions asked in the book, and record the answers. Come up with your own questions, too. A journal is perfect for that.

Please know it is absolutely normal to be tempted to skip some of the steps because you think—at various points—you have it all figured out. Benefiting from *Collateral Happiness* requires assembly of all the information. Just like an IKEA flat-pack shelf unit, when we don't fully complete the steps—will it collapse?— skipping over parts of the book and missing critical detail, or moving on before understanding a section, will result in 'life' forcing you back.

Be patient and gentle with yourself. There's no need to force your way through this guide. You have all the time in the world—your world. Invite each concept to sit for a spell with you; honour and enjoy the process. Make sure you rest during the process. Use those breaks to let your whole-self absorb the information. And, watch out for your ego; it is likely to intervene and insist that you are better than the process.

The quality and length of your journey will be directly connected to your input, your 'point of interest' stops, and your destination. It will be unique to you.

May the road through *Collateral Happiness,* to collateral happiness, lead you to a permanent and peaceful residence, furnished with joy and success on your terms.

The Monologues of the Lower Self

The mindset I now inhabit does not resemble my previous 'life', presented in a series of monologues. This is the depth of suffering from which I arose.

CW

MORNING ROUTINE

Get out of bed.
Go to the washroom.
Wash my hands.
Assess myself in the mirror and think,

Oh Christine, you look fat. UGH.

Head straight to the scale, naked; it's my lightest part of the day.
Stand on the scale.
Look at the number...
147.2

Nooooo.

Instant disappointment.
147.2—yes, point two.

Christine, you are such a failure.
Such a disappointment.
How could you let yourself gain more weight?
Up 19.2 pounds over 3 weeks.
Yes. Nineteen Point Two.
A few weeks ago, in Hawaii, you were 128.

Why can't you eat better?
You are the only one who puts food in your mouth.
You know better.
This shouldn't surprise you.
A bag of chips before bed last night. Why?
You told yourself yesterday that you were going to start your diet.
You said that you were going to have a "good" day.
Now, here we go again.

Okay!
Today I'll try to eat better.
I promise I will.
I hate feeling so fat and looking so gross.
I can't even fit into my fat jeans anymore.
Now what will I wear today?

You are so unworthy and unlovable.
I am so depressed and ashamed.

This was a typical morning. Start the day tuned into 147.2, Radio TBSN, The Burden of Shame Network. An early morning talk show about how I was not good enough.

THE ONE O'CLOCK SHOW

Sit at computer.
Stare at screen.
Open empty calendar.

You have wasted so much of your life.
You have so much education and nothing to show for it.
You have tried so many careers.
You are so unsuccessful. Such a disappointment.
Your resume is a joke.
You keep bouncing around.

No one will ever hire you. You are a reject.
You aren't good enough.
How many attempts are you going to make?
You don't make any money.
You are financially dependent on Scott.
You should have been so much more by now.
How does everyone else get it right?
What is wrong with you?
Yes, feel ashamed.
You thought you were better than this?
You'll never amount to anything.
What's the point of even trying?

This was the 'frequency' that I would dial into to listen to ballads of lack of self-worth and self-deprecation.

EVENING ROUTINE

Kids arrive home.
I long for the daily hug and kiss.
The fighting begins.

You are such a bad parent.
Why do you have to yell at them?
Swearing under your breath? Come on.
You should be volunteering at school.
You should be playing with them.
You should be making more of an effort.
They are going to hate you when they grow up.
Why is everyone else getting it right?
All those FB pictures of others looking so happy.
What is wrong with you?
Why can't you have that?
You are a disgrace. A failure. A waste of space.
Yes, feel ashamed.
Your kids deserve better.
You should never have become a mom.

*Angels, please take my life because I need my mental suffering and anguish to end.
I do not have the courage to do it myself.
I cannot live like this.*

~~~~~

That was my every day. For a long time. I could not find the off-switch.

The List

There came, with the monologues of the lower self, a lengthy want list which included:

Constantly telling myself: 'you have a good life, are a sane person, nothing to complain about.' *Then what is it about?*

Obsessing over my weight and size. My own worst best friend; no one else would ever say as many bad things to me as I did in one day. And I'd never say those things to others. *It's not about the food.*

Wanting to stop procrastinating—too tired, unmotivated—on my career goals. Desperately seeking success. *It's not about the career.*

Longing to stop feeling like a lazy and 'zoned out' mom and wife. *It's not about the external relationships.*

Shrinking away from intimacy because I saw myself as fat and unattractive. *It's not about the food.*

Aching to learn to see myself through my husband's eyes, a man who saw and still sees me, as intelligent, and innovative. *It's not about the external relationships.*

Not wanting to live like that anymore, but not knowing how to change. I knew bits and pieces, but I didn't have a clue how to pull it all together. *It's not about the food, or the career, or external relationships. IT'S ABOUT YOU.*

But a seed of curiosity existed inside me; a feeling that there were answers to be revealed. And I possessed the drive to investigate.

So I began a quest; years of studying, taking courses, talking to people from all walks of life, putting concepts into practice (over time), and painstakingly recording those results, it became clear that it's not about the relationships, career, or the food. It's about intimately understanding one's 'self'. And that requires commitment and hard-work to reach a level of awareness where the benefits are a landscape of collateral happiness comprising:

- releasing weight, permanently and naturally
- developing and maintaining stellar, authentic relationships
- reaching unparalleled levels of personal and professional purpose

Let's Pause

**There is nothing wrong with you.
There is nothing wrong with any of us.**

Isolation makes us think otherwise.
In order to create happiness we require assistance from others,
and we need to know that it is necessary
to ask others for that support.

Breathe.

You can do these steps.
Breathe.

You are so worthy of these changes.

Breathe.

I've got your back.

Hold the book to your heart.

Let me help you prepare to show up for some hard work.

AND

Please know that you are on the way to meeting
the most significant human in your life — you.

Inspiration About Success

You are stronger than you think you are.

If you are saying, "it's too hard, I don't know if I can ever be truly happy", trust me: you can if you choose to.

Struggle is not a crutch or a sign of weakness.

Struggle is our classroom time—our learning. It eventually becomes knowledge and serves as an advantage.

It is our biological requirement for growth and connection. Struggle is not an option but something we must lean into, acknowledge, and move on from.

So, how do we move through our struggles?

- How do we get out of our ruts and climb out from rock bottom?
- How do we each embark on a journey of self-discovery?
- How can we triumph over depression, inertia, low self-worth, or unhappiness?
- How do we each learn to love our self and become our own best friend?
- What steps do we need to take in order to grow?
- How do we create a meaningful life filled with happiness? (Is it even possible?)
- How do we live our best life?
- How do we create a life of fulfillment, living as the best version of our self?

- Why do we choose to eat based on how we look over how we feel?
- Why are we so afraid of things like failure and rejection?
- Why is it so hard to put in the work to be self-aware?
- Why is it so difficult to take the action necessary to achieve higher goals?
- Why do we intentionally and unintentionally hurt others?
- Why do we gossip and talk behind someone's back?
- Why do we want to make fun of someone who isn't like us?
- Why do we withhold support and empathy to those in pain or suffering?

This book will shed light on the answers to these questions, and explain the journey of self-discovery exposed through personal experience, research, and trial and error.

Moving through struggle entails removing ourselves from isolation. Asking for help. Surrounding ourselves with positive influences. Incorporating positive habits. Asking self-reflecting questions. Stopping saying "I can't" is among the results you will discover in this book.

Moving from instant gratification to the appreciation of self-discipline is key. It is through discipline that we build and strengthen our inner being in good times so that we can depend on it to grow and transcend in difficult times.

When we embark on a journey of self-discovery, it is one with no final destination—it's not a race with a finish line. We don't learn how to remove the struggles, we learn how to move through them, each time they occur, with as little suffering as possible.

The only thing standing between you and happy is taking action to change your mindset.

OF FORTUNE TELLERS

Imagine saying to someone...

"Oh, I didn't meet a goal... what a failure."

A failure? For what? For not being a fortune teller and predicting the outcome?

No one knows the future. We can only be certain of our starting point.

Ego sets goals.

Authentic self guides us to reach our best, and beyond.

We learn to live in the law of balance and law of flexibility.

It is in the sweet spot between ego and authentic self that we build strength and discover our true essence of collateral happiness.

To wait or to take longer to achieve our goals means something better is around the corner and is in store.

There are always blessings to be revealed.

We set goals as 'intangible experiences', not tangible experiences.

This is often a difficult concept to accept because of years of conditioning of setting goals and ticking off completion, or beating one's self up for not achieving.

No one is a fortune teller. Incredible outcomes are the results of authentic guidance.

Trust you will get what you **need** and not necessarily what you **want**.

Strive for the best, not mediocrity, even if it takes more time and more effort.

Success comes to those who hold their lives in a patient, harmonic blend of excellence and flexibility.

ANTONYMS

If you look the antonym of goal this is what you get: Aimlessness, avoidance, carelessness, heedlessness, neglect, negligence, oversight, purposelessness, thoughtlessness.

What an eye-opener. It's obvious that people feel horrible about themselves when they do not meet a goal. No wonder we are reticent to set goals.

Such negative undertones.

The thing is, the universe does not see 'goals' that way.

The word goal needs a new definition. One that envelops individuality, authenticity, flexibility, and journey. Any reference to destination should be in tiny print.

The ability to bend brings greater strength than remaining rigid. Engaging patience results in twists and turns that are life altering. For example: how many times do we hear people say, "thank goodness it didn't work out because I would have missed out on …".

We struggle with believing that setting goals leads to exacting results. All or nothing.

Setting goals drives us—there is no doubt. Don't stop envisioning all that excites you and draws you. But, once that's done, release the emotional attachment to a rigid outcome. Instead, keep the engine running and welcome all detours so that you can experience so many more opportunities while 'driving the back roads' to results.

ON GOALS AND WEAKNESSES

Mix up the letters of weakness and there's the word 'awaken'. (Okay, you have to use the 'a' twice.)

It is not weakness to recognize when a goal needs to be reassessed and directions need to be shifted. That's strength. There is a difference between giving up and changing course.

It is weakness to refuse to consider all options and to continue a downward spiral because there is a refusal to adapt and shift. That leads us down the insanity path... doing the same thing, expecting different results.

After you set a goal, continually check in and reassess.

Visualize the steps, not just the goal.

Ask yourself, am I moving along as quickly as I planned? Why not? Is this pace helping me learn? Do I like who I am working with? Am I doing what I planned? If not, then why? What needs to be addressed? What information have I learned, since I started, that is impacting me? Have events outside of my control affected my situation? How do I need to adapt? What can I shift?

We don't always know what we **don't know** when we set a goal. A goal is our guidepost because we are not fortune tellers who predict the future. We take a best guess. Once we establish our goal, we adjust accordingly. We bend and stay flexible to whatever serves us best.

This again is not weakness. This is strength. We use our faith and our instinct, our most valuable tool, to listen to that authentic-self voice. **We get what we need, not always what we want, and so we adapt. We bend.**

Looking back, when things don't go as planned, most of us are grateful for the blessings in disguise. When we are immersed in the change, in the moment, we grasp all threads to stay the course. We view changes as failures to meet goals, rather than seeing changes as blessings. It's a paradox of thoughts.

SUCCESS AND QUALITY

Visualize the process and steps, along with the goal, and then take action. Focus on more than the goal. (Note: there is no finish line.)

So many of us focus all energy on the end goal, the end prize, that we lose focus on what's right in front of us. We lose sight of what it is we need to do today to make that goal reality.

> **Visualizing anything indefinitely won't make it a reality. Progressive action is what achieves outcomes.**

Good things do not come to those who wait. They come to those who work while they wait.

Visualization boards can be action plans that illustrate what we want to achieve—to become—not what we want to 'have'.

Change: So many people get caught in the trap of being really great at keeping busy and spinning in circles. We fool ourselves into thinking we are creating change. Change without progress is really only glorified dabbling in a lot of things, but succeeding in none.

> **Success and quality are not determined by all things that we start, but by all things that we complete.**

It is important to note there are two ways to perceive success:

1. To be concerned only about the satisfaction of succeeding. "I did it". To look only toward the destination.
2. To be concerned about learning, discovery, and maximizing full potential. "I learned". Success emanates from the desire to pursue learning in all its forms, including consequential learning. Developing our mindset and skills helps us achieve our full potential, not necessarily our anticipated success.

Happiness increases with the latter perception, and is dependent upon our awareness.

Ask yourself, am I successful? How many things have I started? Am I just busy? Out of all the things that keep me busy, how many have I actually completed? 'What have I completed' and 'How can I complete this?" What have I learned?

PART II

FOUNDATIONAL UNDERSTANDING OF COLLATERAL HAPPINESS

The Basic Science of the **Body**

The Basic Emotions of the **Mind**

The Approach and Formula for the Creation of Collateral Happiness

The Basics on the Laws of **Spirit** (Human Nature)

Step One:
The Basic Science of the Body

THEORY

You don't have to have aced biology or chemistry to understand this concept. Simply taking in some scientific facts about our human makeup will allow for collateral happiness to unfold.

Our bodies are designed for one thing: survival.

In order to survive, the mind/body sends feelings of pleasure and pain (physical and emotional), of various degrees—depending on the situation—to push or pull us toward survival. The biological response of pleasure and pain also functions in accordance with the law of balance—equalizing polarities as an ebb and flow. It is not static. Not only does our survival depend upon this biological response, so does the quality of our life and the state of our psyche. Healing, growth, and evolution are more effective when balance is achieved.

Our bodies are not designed to default to happiness.

Happiness—true happiness—and the resulting joy and pleasant landscape surrounding it, collateral happiness, is something we work for and then maintain.

To have happiness is to understand, appreciate, and experience balance as a dynamic, opposing force of nature.

The pendulum swing of pleasure and pain is not a biological form of reward and punishment. It is merely an ebb and flow of nature that helps us find balance between the two polarities. Life cannot exist without pain or without struggle. Struggle is a biological requirement for growth and learning. Accepting that struggle is something we learn to manage, not something we attempt to eliminate from our lives.

Happiness is often confused with the temporary state of pleasure. True happiness is a perpetual state of being, where pain and pleasure co-exist as a state of balance. In order to feel genuine happiness, it's necessary to appreciate that it is okay to feel pain, to welcome it as a means of growth, and know that it's imperative to stop seeking external-pleasure as our means of happiness.

When we cease to seek artificial means of pleasure, or believe that pleasure should last indefinitely, we become prime candidates to experience true happiness.

Our biological makeup is this: when we do the things that promote survival, the mind/body rewards us with feelings of pleasure to encourage us to do more of what we are doing. That reward—the feeling of pleasure—is delivered to us in the form of the body's release of neurotransmitters (aka happy hormones): endorphins, serotonin, dopamine, and oxytocin (the latter deemed the cuddle hormone).

When we do things that threaten our survival, we receive signals in the form of pain which travel along the peripheral nervous system to the spinal cord and then the brain. This is a way to discourage and stop us from whatever we are doing. It is the body's way of signaling our brain that we need to stop doing 'those things' for our own protection.

Our bodies are not designed to stay in one state indefinitely.

The body is designed to ebb and flow from negative to positive; basically a graceful balance.

The fine print on our human-science of self: we as a species are driven to expand, micro-evolve, change, and grow—to evolve and progress our centre of balance.

The Basic Science of the Body

To grow means to stretch beyond the limits of comfort as a requirement for personal thriving. Moving beyond levels of comfort can initiate a fear response which we will recognize as pain. Pain, discomfort, and fear are viewed by our intelligent wiring as threats. These threats conflict with the biological response for survival. When survival is threatened, the brain sends out signals for the discomfort or pain to be stopped. The body does not differentiate between pain and fear associated with surviving or thriving.

For example, if a person standing at the edge of a tall building is afraid of falling, or if a person standing in front of a crowd of people is afraid of public speaking, the body's signal of fear and pain is the same; the body's signal is for the person to stop what she is doing.

It's important to note that body's signal of fear and pain is the same (when in fear and pain it says STOP), and yet, in the examples, one action is clearly dangerous and potentially fatal, and the other promotes growth.

This state of discomfort—situated between surviving and thriving—is the key to understanding collateral happiness.

It is a practiced skill to recognize whether pain is a real danger to survival, or if the 'pain' is a requirement for thriving and growing.

This state typically requires assistance from outside positive influences, such as coaches, to help move us past our biological response of wanting to stop the pain, and to guide us through to thriving. This means it is unnatural for people to enjoy change and growth because, associated with pain, the body will send signals to stop as a survival response. In order to embrace change and growth, it is necessary for the mind to override this biological response for survival—to move towards pain, not away from it.

Happiness, growth, and balance are all linked. Since many people lead unhappy lives, it suggests people have not learned to condition the mind for balance and growth, or are not applying the work to do so.

A recent poll, which uses a series of questions to calculate overall happiness, indicates that only 31% of people are 'very happy'. At the same time, about 8 in 10 adults who say they are generally happy with their life right now actually are not, suggesting that people may overstate how happy they really are.

Really, what this means is that people like to say they are happy based on their external circumstances, even though on the inside they feel anything but. We've been conditioned to think that happy is what occurs on the outside; that the outside is right, and how we feel on the inside is mistaken, and thus dismissed.

This is one of life's greatest misconceptions. If we know the external world does not bring us happiness, why do we try to convince ourselves that we are happy basing it on how everything on the outside looks?—good partner, good kids, good home, good job, good friends, good bank account. We should be happy right?

Yet we are not. Happiness is the number one desire of populations worldwide, yet those who have created it are in the minority.

Maybe this means it isn't what we achieve on the outside that determines our happiness; that pleasure created from external circumstance does not define our happiness.

If we base our happiness on external circumstances such as finance, appearance, popularity, consumerism, or instant gratification, we may never experience genuine inner-happiness but only find temporary bursts of pleasure. This is why food, particularly sugar, or other habitual substances have become the perfect artificial happiness "fix". They are external, and they are an instant way to produce the release of happy hormones, misleading us into thinking we are happy.

The Basic Science of the Body

Food, drugs, or other dependencies artificially inflate our state of pleasure with the release of neurotransmitters as a distraction to the real problems in our life. The temporary bursts of pleasure from these substances will never lead to genuine inner-happiness.

SIMPLE SCIENCE, COMPLEX BODIES

Food is no longer sourced or produced as it was when our ancestors lived. Today offers a world of choices that include natural and unnatural; a range comprising over-processed products with little nutrition. Consumption of these processed foods, particularly sugar, can artificially inflate our neurotransmitters (aka happy hormones): dopamine, serotonin, and endorphins.

> Neurotransmitters: chemical messengers that coordinate the transmission of signals from one nerve cell (neuron) to the next.
>
> These all important brain chemicals interact with target sites, called receptors, which are located throughout the brain (and body) to regulate a wide variety of processes including emotions, fear, pleasure, joy, anger, mood, memory, cognition, attention, concentration, alertness, energy, appetite, cravings, sleep, and the perception of pain.
>
> Neurotransmitters chemically link the brain and spinal cord with the rest of the body: muscles, organs, and glands. Thus, our brain is not only an array of wires (nerve cells/neurons) but also a highly evolved chemical soup (neurotransmitters).
>
> Neurotransmitters affect every cell, tissue, and system in your body. And because neurotransmitters are functionally integrated with the immune system and the endocrine system (including the adrenal glands), neurotransmitter imbalances can cause widespread health problems.
> (https://www.integrativepsychiatry.net/neurotransmitter.html)

Collateral Happiness: The Power Behind the Facade

Foods greatly influence the brain's behavior. A poor diet is a common cause of neurotransmitter imbalance. Neurotransmitters which regulate our behavior are controlled by what we eat. What we eat affects mood. When the brain produces serotonin, tension is eased. When it produces dopamine, we tend to think and act more quickly and feel more alert.

Eating complex carbs—oatmeal, brown rice, quinoa, potatoes, beans, peas and lentils—increases serotonin levels, which then creates a calming effect. Eating high protein foods—eggs, chicken, fish, beef, nuts, beans—promotes dopamine production which boosts alertness. (Summarized from: *Prescription for Nutritional Healing*, Phyllis A. Balch, CNC.)

For example, sitting in front of the TV with carbs like chips, pasta, and chocolate can feel soothing after a stressful day. Eating protein like trail mix and a chicken salad can make us feel more attentive before a big exam.

Think about the chocolate bar or colourful candies you pick up whenever you're at a certain store—you know the packaging intimately because you've searched it out in unfamiliar shops. You recognize and respond to those sweet-treats that you sometimes stockpile in fear that the manufacturer will stop making them.

This need for that food is called a food craving or false hunger, and it can be the result of an imbalance of serotonin: leading to that kind of feeling that 'nothing is good enough'. But, more often than not, we temporarily satisfy our cravings with artificial fixes.

Cravings are our mind-body-soul's way of expressing that we need more than an artificial fix.

No matter how great an experience, without the necessary serotonin required to create the feeling of satisfaction, a person is left wanting more.

Or in the circumstance of too much dopamine, a person is left with the feeling of wanting more without knowing what it is he or she wants more of.

The production of endorphins can help inhibit or muffle pain signals.

Alcohol, drugs, gambling, and food can all fire up the reward pathway to heights that we cannot achieve naturally.

Intense behaviors—that ecstatic joy we create artificially—takes over the limbic system, that primitive and crucial part of our brain, resulting in a massive production of 'happy hormones'; an artificial high experienced in the euphoria of intoxication.

When food, drugs, or something else, gains entry to the brain and provides immediate gratification, a quick fix, it is not a natural high—not the results of natural causes.

Sugar is anchored in the core of food addiction. Eating processed sugar produces an unnatural experience which results in an artificial high from the product—a far more powerful 'high' than that which a natural high would provide.

Can you see how this leads us to recognizing, and then takes us toward understanding, the science of addiction?

The 'high' is unrestrained. It is artificial. Over the top. Natural means cannot deliver such levels of this powerful stimulant. And it is not just food.

We become enslaved easily by that which creates an unnatural high.

And when we cut off that source of the unnatural high, we crash. Our human GPS is then set for anxiety, depression, and other disruptive and dangerous routes.

In *Staying Healthy with Nutrition,* by Elson M. Haas, MD, says:

> Although sugar addiction is common, sugar withdrawal is usually physically mild, with periodic strong cravings. The most difficult part for many is making the decision to stop sugar use, and this is because of the emotional attachments to sugar. For those who are sensitive to refined sugar or sweeteners, or who consume it in large amounts, genuine symptoms of abuse and withdrawal may also occur. Some of these symptoms include fatigue, anxiety and irritability, depression and detachment, rapid heart rate and palpitations, and poor sleep. Most symptoms, if they do occur, last only a few days… Once sugar has been removed from the diet, it is still possible to use it once in a while, as it is not as re-addicting as many stronger drugs. Most people who have kicked the sugar habit find that they no longer tolerate sugar very well.

This helps explain that food cravings are not actually a lack of willpower but a physiological process. So hear this:

There is nothing wrong with you.

Hear it as if I have shouted it from the rooftops in your community. There is nothing wrong with you.

On the subject of overeating and weight-loss, at some point there is work to be done to make the decision to cut or limit sugar (and excess simple carbs), from your routine. But when that decision is made, it will be with an understanding of the process of creating inner-happiness, and a basic outline of the science.

When we understand why we are doing the work it makes the tasks easier to carry out. When we comprehend the process we do not feel deprived; we feel empowered.

So, yes, cravings will occur as the body detoxes from high-levels of sugar. A protest of sorts. During the absence of sugar, the body cries out for that 'artificial' high it has become used to.

The Basic Science of the Body

Once detoxed from sugar, cravings for certain foods will dissipate. Once the cravings ease, it is easier to establish a peaceful relationship with food.

And the same is true when stopping or limiting other artificial highs. The science applies to them all: the overspending, gambling, drugs, television, alcohol, over-exercising—all forms of 'unnatural and instant gratification' which is extreme.

To achieve a life of inner-happiness, which will produce a healthy body weight, a strengthened immune system, peace and clarity of mind, and other benefits, it's essential to understand HOW to create natural happiness (leaving artificial happiness in the dust).

- Does it mean eliminating 'stuff' you enjoy? No.
- Does it mean you will never play poker again? No.
- Does it mean you can never watch a television series? Of course not.

When you experience yourself in a state of not having those artificial highs and those overindulgences that were borderline obsession or addiction, you will be able to understand the science of the matter; that "cravings" are not actually a message that says you lack willpower, but a physiological process that shows how reliant your body was on certain things, and how habitual those things have become.

The road to becoming authentically happy is achieved in small steps; incremental changes that add up to total transformation. And that route begins with healthier foods.

If we remove the substances that artificially inflate our happy hormones, it is then necessary to learn and understand how to create 'natural' happiness, from within, in order to prevent a return to dependency on artificial means of happiness.

This biological range—naturally experiencing levels of pleasure and pain—is a key design in our bodies for survival, and for improvement.

In order for us, as humans today, to achieve goals, we know there will be 'growing pains' of sorts. Put simply: some discomfort. At these times, with our eye on the prize, when we are working hard, we will receive signals of discomfort—the body saying "you might not survive so stop doing this". This is when people often quit or overload.

This process was much simpler when we lived simple lives.

It was a breeze when there were no ivory towers complete with political power struggles and fights for promotions; when there were no such things as corner convenience stores stocked with processed products.

Life in the past, though harsh in some respects, was extremely straightforward; our relationships functioned through cooperation and the relatively uncomplicated lifestyle of hunting and gathering.

We now live in a society in which technology is advancing at such a rapid pace most cannot keep up—and maintain a calm balance—social media influences our moods, relief comes in the form of thirty-ingredient foods, thirty-lettered additives, thirty cigarettes in a pack, thirty ounces in a bottle, thirty outlet stores in a compound, thirty fun-filled days on the tour of your lifetime with all you can eat buffets and all-inclusive packages of paradise.

We live in a world of over-abundance in which society encourages instant gratification to escape the busy-ness or 'issues' of every day.

And here's the problem with these forms of release.

They are artificial. And they are temporary.

The brain has a way of dealing with a temporary fix. The reward centre kicks in, no doubt about it, and it sends pleasurable feelings. The body says, "You are doing something that makes me send you rewards in the way of pleasurable feelings; that is good—it means you are surviving, so keep doing what you are doing."

What you are doing is via an artificial stimulus. You are fooling your body into handing out pleasurable feelings.

Here lies the problem: after a certain amount of time, whatever you are buying, consuming, inhaling, or injecting is not enough for the brain. It wants more. The signaling centre gets used to that amount of artificial stimulation, and demands more in order to reach the same levels of 'happy' continuously. The pleasurable feelings are not that pleasurable unless you do more buying, inhaling, injecting, or consuming.

Having the belief we should live in the moment and do things that make us feel good right now creates a false sense of wellbeing. It is an illusion.

There are further complications. After the artificially induced pleasure is experienced, there follows a substantial drop—a low. If the body is 'fed' more of whatever induced the artificial happiness, so that it can keep up pleasurable feelings, the system becomes overburdened by receiving more (chemical) stimulus than the brain was designed to handle.

Artificially tampering with the body's release of happy hormones leads to myriad issues, from addiction to depression.

DEFINITIONS

Internal happiness: the near-constant flow of joy we feel that is not affected by external circumstances. A state we create from our own actions, thoughts, and beliefs. A blissful peace that takes place in the balanced mind, body, and soul.

Examples: feeling a warm wave of gratitude when the wind blows through our hair, no matter our geographic location; the serenity of inhaling the scent of a flower; the pride we feel from having grown our own vegetables.

External happiness: the temporary state of pleasant feelings we enjoy when something happens in our outer world. A supercharging, superficial, arousal—much like the eruption of a fireworks display, and its subsequent conclusion.

Examples: the rush we get when we overindulge in alcohol; the high from booking a tropical vacation; the excitement we feel on an impulsive, expensive purchase.

Collateral happiness: state of inner fulfillment and joy created as a result of overcoming struggle, embracing discomfort and applying discipline which creates an outward ripple effect of happiness.

MORE ABOUT US

Fear not, it's not rocket science. And you don't have to read this all in one sitting.

If this is new information for you, take your time with it. If it's not new, don't let your ego tell you to skip this section.

Today's society has conditioned us to expect pleasure all the time; anything less and society delivers the message that we are failures.

Society's messages confuse us because we indulge in stimulants that are unnatural. We have instant gratification at our fingertips and can receive excessive pleasure at the click of a button or the swipe of a card.

Take eating, for example. Our ancestors did not always know where their next meal was coming from but, when there was food, it was natural. But today, given the copious amounts of processed food available, when we eat so much that it makes us feel uncomfortable, we start to experience physical pain. The body is telling us to stop. The body's biological response is seeking balance, not excess.

The range of natural happiness is much more satisfying than wild swings of high-pleasure, followed by extreme-discomfort—lows which continue to plunge, over time, if we do not sustain the pleasure.

We've lost the reference for this delicate balancing act of pleasure and discomfort. Think: all you can eat buffets, all-inclusive vacations with unlimited alcohol, super-sized meals containing little nutrition. Think: two-for-one sales, buy now pay later, have this product delivered tomorrow. Then consider this: graceful balance does not sell, and does not make a profit.

Examples of artificial stimuli are: overeating, consuming certain foods, alcohol, or drugs, excessive shopping, smoking, over-exercising, overspending on vacations for instant gratification and status.

Do we do what is easy and makes us feel good right now in the moment or do we do what is necessary and difficult—though uncomfortable—in order to create greater happiness down the road?

Each of us arrives at our own answer.

There is no right or wrong. **There is only cause and effect.**

One choice will result in artificial and temporary moments of pleasure, the other choice provides an outcome which can be described as an ongoing state of peace, joy, and calm which is the embodiment of collateral happiness.

When people lean into the discomfort, knowing that it is necessary for growth, and allowing their vulnerability to expose them to connection, the need for the artificial 'stuff' diminishes, even disappears. The connections generated from 'self work' creates genuine inner-happiness; a feeling of transcendence.

This feeling is a natural biological response. **When people experience inner-happiness they no longer need the artificial fix.**

REVIEW AND TAKEAWAYS

Happiness is a by-product created from our own action. It is not something we 'find' but something we radiate. It is not a goal, it is a result.

When we no longer artificially inflate our happy hormones, we begin to learn how to address the pain we are seeking to avoid, and figure out how to feel pleasure naturally. We can then take back a healthy power of choosing what we put in our mouths, how we move our bodies, and what we inhale.

The creation of inner-happiness is a learned skill; ongoing training applied consistently over time.

And as we develop natural happiness—taking the time to focus on our whole self—we free up time and space to dig into the root of our behaviours, make peace with them, reset the journey.

There is nothing wrong with you. If you think there is, it just means you have not learned the science of survival.

- Our bodies are designed for survival, not happiness.
- Pain threatens survival. Pleasure encourages it.
- Pain and pleasure co-exist as a natural ebb and flow in nature.
- In order to live, we are required to grow.

The Basic Science of the Body

- Growth causes a discomfort that feels like pain.
- Survival instincts signal the body to stop the pain.
- If we suppress pain and discomfort, and artificially inflate happy hormones to create pleasure, we create disharmony in the body: physically, mentally, and emotionally.
- To experience joy as a result of growth, we accept that the payment for it is overcoming the pain, not eliminating it.
- We can become adept at recognizing the difference between pain as a real threat to survival, and when it is necessary for growth.

KEY QUESTION

Is attaining the perfect house, the perfect family, the perfect job and the perfect appearance seeking pleasure or creating happiness?

PRACTICAL PRACTICE

Doing what is difficult, uncomfortable and disciplined creates a life of happiness. Doing what is easy, comfortable and undisciplined creates a life of misery.

Take a few moments to list or think about the artificial, temporary fixes you include in your current life... don't worry about them, just note them.

Don't try to think about what non-temporary fixes you should be replacing them with. Not right now. Just focus and lean into the discomfort.

> Breathe, rest, hold the book to your heart.
> Move to Step Two when you are truly ready.

Step Two:
The Basic Emotions of the Mind

ESSENTIALS

✓ You've got a handle on the science of you, those basics of neurotransmitters.

✓ You've accepted that **there is nothing wrong with you.**

With that done, we can move forward to a discussion on emotions. No prerequisite in psychology required. You've got all you need to dive into the topic.

So, what is emotion?

Professor Google says:
> a natural instinctive state of mind deriving from one's circumstances, mood, or relationships with others.
> "she was attempting to control her emotions"
> Synonyms: feeling, sentiment, reaction, response.

Emotions are always present, but surges of emotion zip in and out and can be extreme—pleasure or pain. Regardless of whether emotions are positive or negative, they are driven by reasoning abilities, and levels of perception.

States of feeling bring about psychological changes and physical changes that affect our behavior, the nervous system being aroused.

Emotion is related to motivation.

What does this mean? Well, if we want to find motivation, which is a feeling, to change our outcome we need to understand how emotion fits into the equation.

By default, our **outcomes** are generated by our **actions**. Our actions are driven by our emotions. Emotions are created from our subconscious or conscious **thoughts**. Thoughts are formed through our external **influences and stimuli**.

Since feelings are temporary, motivation is temporary. For this reason it is vital to understand how to use influences to continually drive motivation.

Taking action and making changes requires an intimate understanding of our emotions and what drives them.

When it comes to dis-ease and dis-comfort of any kind—physical or mental—our bodies are finite containers.

That means limited.

We can only hold so much 'stress' before we crash and burn.

Neither can we hold opposite emotions at the same time. Emotions take up space, especially negative emotions. When we choose to hold on to a negative, it finds a place to take up residence, and it sits inside us and toxifies the area surrounding it. We see the results of this in self-destructive behaviour, poor attitude, and manifestation of illness.

When we hold on to many negatives, the vessel that we are cannot be topped up with positives. Negative tends to invite negative, whether through thought patterns, practices, or even the people we choose to hang out with.

Here's a startling image of how negative emotions have built-up and all but choked off perfectly worthy feelings—we're all valued, we're all enough, we're all capable.

```
         GRATITUDE
           PRIDE              ┐
       ABANDONMENT            │   20% Positive Body
         JEALOUSY              
          GREED                
       RESENTMENT             │   80% Negative Body
          ANGER                
          SHAME               
          GUILT               ┘
```

When we are filled with mostly negative emotions and, for various reasons, continue to hold on to them, we cannot achieve a positive balance, feel much joy, or easily move forward.

It takes an investment in ourselves to first become aware and acknowledge each negative emotion we hold—resulting from thoughts or beliefs—so that we can identify the source and allow ourselves the choice to release that negative emotion and free up space for positives.

Self-discipline means to control one's emotions; to invest in the self and care for the self.

Erase your thoughts of 'the ruler over the knuckles in school' scenario. Get rid of wearing a forty-pound backpack and hiking five miles with a drill sergeant on your tail. Clear your mind of any kind of deprivation, and forget everything you associate with discipline.

Fresh thoughts.

Discipline means to practice and control.

Discipline is not a bad word.

For that we need a clear mindset and a re-education on food, movement, meditation, connection, and the value of learning.

A break from the emotional theory. How are you doing? Let's take an interlude.

~~Let's pause on understanding emotions for a moment~~

WILL IT HURT?

While you work to create collateral happiness—will it hurt?

Yes. But the discomfort that comes with 'pain' will result in something invaluable coming out of your actions.

It's when we feel most uncomfortable that there is the opportunity for deep reflection—that's where the real growth happens.

As humans, we do best with steps. One thing at a time.

HOW CAN I MEASURE MY PROGRESS?

In society, we are praised for multi-tasking, we brag about how much we accomplish in a day, and are chastised because we have not reached our 'goals'.

Small steps are not currently trending in society. Small steps are rarely recognized, therefore not taken, because they are not honoured.

We are not socialized to express our celebration of self over small steps; in fact, such acknowledgement seems to emphasize our weaknesses and issues.

This has to stop.

We have a ceremony at graduation, but during those 80-minute classes, study periods, lectures, essays, intimidating tests, and projects, we simply toil. We party only when we reach certain milestones, yet ignore, almost hide, those steps that led to those milestones.

Celebration of small steps is essential to normalizing natural happiness.

We need to get used to celebrating small steps. For it is the culmination of all the things we do which gives us the whole.

Please give yourself permission to cheer that you have reached this page. Please pat yourself on the back for having read some paragraphs twice, or made some notes in the margins, or written in a journal when you identified with a concept—when something touched your heart.

Clap, dance, shout, sing your praises, hug someone, cry or just do whatever feels good. There's no need to prolong enjoying your success until a final moment. Reaching a state of true inner-happiness requires the opposite: the recognition and celebration of small steps, for there is no finish line, only natural happiness (which, as mentioned, produces healthier minds, bodies, more creativity, stronger immune systems, deeper connections).

Still questioning your commitment. Hey, you've done Step One.

HOW DO I KNOW IF I'M READY?

Life is what happens when we are participating in it not just planning it.

What were you planning when you picked up this book? What might get in the way of staying with this book? With me? When we rely on external happiness and then life happens, it is rarely our definition of perfect. So, then what do we do? Do we put happiness aside until those days blow over? What if those days never blow over?
You may be second guessing that you don't have it in you to do the work. You may feel cynical that this will be a waste of time—or that you will fail. That's the whole point of these first pages: to express that the steps to inner-happiness take time and that

there is more to it than just making a decision. But, if not now, when?

Inner-happiness can be experienced even when the kids are crying, when we lack sleep, when the boss is a jerk. We just choose to make one choice at a time to learn the concept.

A state of inner-happiness improves our immune system, helps us become more creative, releases weight. When we establish a state of inner-happiness we never have to run from our weight. We don't have to hide from difficult conversations or mask our anger. Arriving at a state of inner-happiness places us in the position of engaging a sort-of super power that resembles peaceful control.

And over time, you will see that super-power emerge, step-by-step.

There is absolutely no need to wait until we are wealthy, promoted, and/or skinny to be happy. We can have it right now. The daily application of seemingly small, perhaps even boring, things (as listed in the happiness formula) will ensure the creation of genuine happiness unfolds for you.

At this point, you may be getting the idea that this is a long haul —and that you might get frustrated. Maybe you want to ask yourself again: Do I want to be happy? Sit with that idea. Look around for signs of why you want to make the changes. Then make the choice whether to move on.

Picture yourself with me, Christine the life coach, even though we're face to page.

HOW IS THIS BOOK DIFFERENT THAN AN IN-PERSON LIFE COACH?

That depends on how committed you are to keeping this book beside you, opening it on a regular basis, and moving through the steps.

I intend for the book to help enlighten you by providing insight. The book, with its theory and anecdotal aspects are as close to an in-person coach as I can create on paper.

Book or person, you'll still need to be accountable to yourself. An in-person coach can be a face-to-face reminder to keep you accountable, challenge your beliefs, ask you questions you would not think to ask, urge you to do your homework, help guide you through surviving to thriving, and—most importantly—be there to support, cheer, and hug you through your journey.

UP CLOSE AND PERSONAL
(Between You and Me)

If you were in my office, and this was our first meeting, and I'd explained about the brain science of us, the inner-happiness versus external artificial happiness, and what my role is, I would ask you one very straightforward question that would determine if I would take you on as a client: **are you committed and invested in creating collateral happiness?**

I'm asking you that now. Are you? Are you committed and invested?

You might only be interested. And being interested is different.

There is no right or wrong answer. Being interested means you are not quite ready. Being committed means you are.

Imagine you are standing at the altar ready to exchange marriage vows with your fiancé, and the minister asks your fiancé, "Do you take this person as your partner for the rest of your life?"
Now imagine that your fiancé replies, "Yes, I am 98% committed." 98% is a great number, a high percentage. Would you marry someone willing to commit to you 98% or do you want the 100%? That is the difference. Commitment is 100% and interested is 99% or less. Commitment does not mean being 'perfect' and always getting things right. It only means you are determined to succeed and willing to make the effort to learn.

Why is this such an important question to me?

Because I do not want to set you up to fail.

Once it gets hard, difficult and boring, which it will, if you are only interested you will quit. Why? Because motivation is temporary. I have the steps to help you create collateral happiness, but I cannot walk them for you. I can, and will, guide you and hold your hand in support, but you must be willing to take each step. You are responsible for your success. And the payment for success —ultimately to collateral happiness—is overcoming discomfort, creating discipline, and accepting struggle.

Are you willing to take the first step?

Remember you don't have to do this alone.

How many more days do you wish to waste?

And know it is never too late.

Know that, when you commit, there will be some slip-ups, but each day will get better. Lessons and learning. Progress.

~~Getting back to understanding the emotions~~

Cognitively, we have two brains. The 'emotional brain' and the 'thinking brain'.

We are wired to default to emotional systems—our actions are determined by the emotional system first.

Influences and stimuli alter the emotional and thinking brains.

According to New York University brain scientist, Joseph LeDoux, "Connections from the emotional systems to the cognitive (thinking) systems are stronger than connections from the cognitive systems to the emotional systems."

The emotional brain is part of the limbic system, the portion of the brain that controls emotions, memories, and arousal (or stimulation). One of the chief responsibilities for the limbic system is survival; another is memory access and storage.

The subconscious mind is located in the limbic system, which has the capacity to multitask. This gives us the ability to make quick decisions. While the thinking brain is at rest, the emotional brain is at work helping us to solve problems and uncover opportunities. It nudges us into doing things or not doing things.

This system is driven by pain and pleasure. It subconsciously affects our behavior in the pattern of emotional response. It responds to pleasure as inner peace and balance. It reacts to threats as an instinct for survival mode—and reports those threats to us through fear or pain. The stronger your feeling is toward a certain event or experience, the stronger your reaction.

The thinking brain includes the prefrontal cortex—the portion of the brain which mediates decision making, voluntary thought, awareness, self-control, and planning. This part of the brain can only perform one function at a time. (When we multitask we are actually switching from one part of the brain to another.)

This is where willpower and our ability to focus consciously for short periods of time reside. Multitasking (switching from one part of the brain to another) and deep conscious thinking tires the brain. When the 'brains' are tired, the default response to any stimuli will be from the emotional brain. Sometimes we refer to this as turning on our 'auto-pilot'.

Put simply: as humans, we are wired for the 'emotional brain' to overrule the thinking brain.

The good news is that we can override this response. The thinking brain is able to mute our emotional brain. It's just not instinctive, natural, or easy. **The goal is to learn to take a conscious thought, overriding the emotional brain and subconscious**

thoughts, and then to take action even if we don't feel like it.

For example, it rarely feels good to exercise. The pain, sweat, and deep breathing are turn offs. This is when having a coach or trainer can be beneficial to help you use the thinking brain to override the emotional brain. You know it won't 'feel' good in the moment, but choose to persist and do it anyways because the result will feel good. It is natural to not 'feel' like exercising. It's just not an excuse.

Changing the brain's default pathway (from the emotional limbic system to the cognitive thinking cortex) is achievable. To get the brain's cortex to tell the limbic system what to do requires a plethora of practices, including:
- the formulation of positive habits
- a release of negative emotions and self-limiting beliefs
- using a coach, mentor or trainer
- using positive and pleasurable associations with the thought

Below are some quick, short-term strategies that can be implemented to turn on the thinking brain:

1. **Stop and Go.** We literally say, "Stop" to the emotional brain, and say, "Go" to the thinking brain.

2. **Countdown.** We can count down like a rocket ship launch where we transition emotional brain to thinking brain.

3. **Make some noise.** Startling sounds or loud noises can trigger a switch in emotional and thinking brains. Play a short siren or drumroll to turn on the thinking brain. Think: pregame warm-up.

4. **Sing.** We can play a motivational song and sing to it, and then tell the brain to turn the thinking brain on.
   Examples include:

- James Brown – I Feel Good
- Eminem – Lose Yourself or Not Afraid
- AC/DC – Thunderstruck
- Journey – Don't Stop Believing
- Bon Jovi – It's My Life
- Gloria Gaynor – I Will Survive
- The Heavy – How Do You Like Me Now?

5. **Question.** Ask questions to trigger the thinking brain to tune in. Who am I impacting? What do I want and need? Why must I change? When can I commit? How much more time am I willing to waste?

6. **Visualize.** Picture, in your mind's eye, the back of the brain quieting and shrinking while the front of the brain opens and enlarges. Envision the front of the brain in charge, at the podium, microphone greenlighted.

Are you ready? Why or why not?

Is your brain starting to hurt after reading this? If so, that is good. That means you are turning on the thinking brain. The brain is like your heart and needs to be conditioned and worked.

Keeping the emotional brain from continually taking over comes down to learning how to release stored negative emotions and beliefs.

That means decision-making, commitment to understanding the various steps we can take to let go of negatives, and, ultimately, the application of those steps/lessons.

Emotions such as guilt, rejection, and jealousy take up space that could be used to experience the feelings of innocence, connection, and compassion.

The process of release takes discipline. Yes, discipline. Please don't stop here. At least read the next statement.

The Basic Emotions of the Mind

If we choose to live in ignorance or avoidance it is choosing to live with our heads in the sand; nothing above ground changes.

We cannot speak away the emotions we wish to release.

- First, we must identify and acknowledge the emotion we want to release.
- Next, it's essential to introduce a stronger positive to counter the negative.

In order to feel something, we have to believe that feeling. In order to believe something we rely on having been influenced. This is why we each of us have individual beliefs about the same thing; our beliefs depend upon past influence.

As babies, we come into this world with no beliefs other than the distress of falling and loud noises. It is through worldly conditioning that we formulate our beliefs, over time. It is those beliefs that impact our emotions.

Ultimately: if a negative belief is formed by influence, a negative emotion will result. The only way to change the emotion is by introducing a new positive influence that will create a new positive belief. To say an affirmation is not enough.

For example, many clients come to me feeling guilt. I cannot help them release guilt until I explain to them that, when they made the choice to act, it was without them knowing the consequence —they did not have 20/20 vision.

I explain there is no judgment. Those with feelings of guilt are not the same people they once were. Their current values (not the values they had in the past) affect perception.

In order to help someone release the feeling of guilt, I work as the influence who disrupts the current story and belief they tell themselves. After I influence the interruption of the current story of guilt, then the person can begin the process of releasing the feeling of guilt. To tell someone, "just stop feeling guilty," is not effective on its own.

This is why when I say, "we cannot speak our feelings into action", it is because we must first address the situation with a positive influence which can change our belief—our story. It is almost impossible to change without some sort of positive external influence.

The key is investing in ourselves to find awareness of the negative emotion that needs to be released, and employing discipline to learn the skill of how to release that emotion. When we make the choice to release it, we still need to follow it with an appropriate action. If we don't know the action, it's imperative that we take the time and effort to learn what action is needed.

When we make choices to release negative emotion, and take action to replace our containers with positive emotion, the results have a snowball effect—a flow of positive enters through the higher-self.

Releasing negatives is not just speaking the words into existence, but preceding those words with a positively inspired influence.

Releasing of negative emotions is a skill; totally learnable.

Not releasing negatives increases the chances of numbing out and interjecting an artificial state (television, shopping, food) of happiness. Once we honor the negative emotion, whether it be jealousy or feeling left out, we can finally begin to work on its release and our freedom.

> *Just living is not enough...*
> *one must have sunshine, freedom and a little flower.*
>
> Hans Christian Anderson

The Basic Emotions of the Mind

At this stage we are simply learning about the laws of emotions. Later on, we'll focus on how nutrition, movement, meditation, connection, learning, and other habits help the mind-body-soul release negative emotion.

UNDERSTANDING NEGATIVE EMOTIONS

Pain—discomfort—is not meant to be something bad that we avoid or run from. It is not intended to affect our lives indefinitely. Pain is an indicator of growth, and it works in accordance with the law of balance for our survival.

It is a signal from our body for something to change.

Humans have turned 'pain' into meaning something bad. Pain is not bad; it is an effect. Negative emotions are really a 'call to action' or a 'need for a change' in direction or belief.

Emotional pain is our body telling us that what we are currently doing is not working.

What triggers our emotions? Our thoughts/beliefs and our influences.

THE PAIN SIGNALS—EXCESS BAGGAGE

If we want to have positive emotions, we can work to create an environment of positive influences and thoughts.

Negative emotions are created from negative external circumstances. This means we can only release them by experiencing positive external circumstances. It is vital that we make those positives happen rather than wait for them to happen to us.

a. **Shame** signals that we think that there is something wrong with us and our individual identity. *I am bad, I am a failure.* To overcome shame, the self-limiting belief driving the emotion has to be changed. We can do this by sharing—with trusted others—whatever it is that we are ashamed of. Opening up frees us from hiding secrets, allowing forward movement. Releasing shame brings a sense of freedom to the soul.

b. **Guilt** signals that we think we did something bad. *I did something bad. I failed.* But we do not think we ARE bad or a failure. It is an action and does not become a part of our identity. Guilt signals that we violated a personal expectation. It is an attachment to our ideal self as opposed to our real self.

c. **Humiliation** signals that we don't think we deserve to be treated poorly when we have, in fact, perceived that we have been treated poorly. *She called me stupid and I didn't deserve that.*

d. **Embarrassment** signals that we did something silly, but other people have done *something silly* too, so we don't take it on as our identity.

e. **Fear** signals that we are uncertain of the future and are unprepared. We cannot predict the future so there is no point in trying. We can stop focusing all attention on the risk and shift focus onto the reward. We can also focus on learning.

f. **Failure** signals that we did not achieve what we expected. Failure is alleviated quickly by exchanging the word failure with learn. *I have now learned what not to do; let's get back to figuring out what to do.* We can also detach ourselves emotionally from expected outcomes and invite the lessons in.

g. **Rejection** signals that we think we are not worthy of love and connection. It may even threaten our existence.

h. **Emptiness** signals a sense that our core human needs or birthrights are unfulfilled or we lack meaning in life.

i. **Anger** signals that a rule or value has been violated.

j. **Frustration** signals that an expectation has not been met and that we think we can do something better than what has been done; we just choose to change our approach.

k. **Disappointment** signals that we expected more than what we got, or that a goal is not going to happen. We can remind ourselves to take control of our individual self rather than wait for things to happen.

l. **Inadequacy** signals that we don't have the skill or craft yet to be what we desire to be.

m. **Loneliness** signals that we feel we don't have anyone in our life who cares about us—that we lack deep emotional connection with others.

n. **Boredom** manifests as a lack of meaning in one's life, repressed creative energy, or a lack of adventure and variety.

REVIEW AND TAKEAWAYS

Step One and Two overviewed a great deal of science of addiction and touched on emotions. The concept of celebrating small steps was emphasized. Below, in PRACTICAL PRACTICE, you will be asked about **your** emotional state.

This is a huge ask.

- Influence + Thoughts (subconscious and conscious) + Feelings + Actions = Results
- Are we committed or are we interested?
- We can only allow positive emotions in by creating space, removing the negative emotions.

KEY QUESTIONS

If I am only interested in creating collateral happiness, what is keeping me from being fully invested and totally committed?

What do I ultimately want?

Can I answer the question: who am I?

What emotions are preventing you from getting what you want? What beliefs are driving those emotions? What influenced you to create that belief? Is that belief currently serving you?

Take your time in thinking about these questions and your answers.

Proceed slowly. Go back if you need to. Draw pictures if that comes easier than expressing yourself in words.

If you do not know the answers yet, that is okay. The first step of the process is creating awareness of what you know and what you do not know.

This is not an essay competition, bullet points are fine.

Make notes in your journal. There is no timer running or competition with others. This is your journey. We each absorb information at different rates. The first two steps on the road to inner-happiness, to creating a landscape of inner-happiness are done. Kudos to you.

Let's go a little deeper, then move on to the formula I created for creating collateral happiness.

The Basic Emotions of the Mind

PRACTICAL PRACTICE

To the left side of the image, below, identify your current negative emotions and beliefs. Then use the space to the right side of the image to identify your current positive emotions and beliefs.

Note: it is difficult to be a positive person if your container is filled with more negative than positive. Is yours? If it is, know that it is unproductive to keep beating yourself up for not being perfect. You are not a bad person. Instead, make the choice to take the steps required to remove the negative emotions.

You are absolutely capable of stopping the blame-game—blaming everyone (thing) else for your problems—and can immediately start taking responsibility for your own happiness.

Negative   Positive

This Is Jane

A few weeks ago, discipline was like a swear word to me.

I didn't understand that discipline meant investing in myself. Didn't get it meant following my higher-self.

In fact, the higher-self sounded a bit woo-woo to me.

A few weeks ago I'd never have said: "I'm going for a walk today." And I don't mean a stroll with the kids—both under ten—but a brisk walk by myself.

Until recently, the slick running shoes, an 'old' New Year's resolution, were still price-tagged and bound together by an unbreakable nylon thread through the eyelets.

It'd been a long time since I'd felt freedom and confidence; seven years since I'd left the work force—no! Nine, almost ten. I just felt kind of numb. I wasn't even sure what the point of waking up each day was. I charged my batteries with coffee, donuts, and fast food, and managed to watch every episode of *Suits* at least twice.

Moments of clarity were rare; too busy grabbing fistfuls of guilt over not being a good enough mom to my son and daughter, not being a desirable enough wife, not being a professional anything. Every day I gained weight and lost more of me.

When, a few weeks ago, I met with a life coach, Grace, she told me, right up front, that there was nothing wrong with me.

I wanted to believe her, but I knew there was a lot wrong with me—even started listing it out loud for her. But, she wasn't having any of it. She backed up her statement with facts about the brain and about emotions; presented a pretty strong case. She offered a practical approach that impressed me. No woo-woo.

There was nothing wrong with me.

What a relief.

What a fricking massive, humongous relief. Grace gave me hope. And, boy was I eager to take the pill that would turn it all around. Ready for the magic potion. I could almost taste the elixir of life.

Ten seconds later, she said she was going to encourage me to move. I hoped she meant house, because the last thing I wanted to do was exercise. I even asked her if she was mistaken and had meant to say 'diet' not 'exercise'.

To me, exercise was for those who already had their lives together—for those who wore sports-bras as pop-tops, and whose perky butts resembled firm bounce-a-coin-off-ness.

I looked around Grace's office for a shelf of supplements and protein powders. All I saw was my sorry reflection in a mirror with an etched edge—the kind one sees above a granny's fireplace. I even pleaded a little bit: "Can't I just cut out some sugar and have some meals delivered, then promise not to eat anything but what is in the program's package?"

Apparently going to a life coach is not like going to a 'diet centre'. There is no food program, and there are no packages of prepared foods. There's not even a scale. There are no groups of women comparing stories of weekly losses and gains.

There is me. There is Grace. There is a box of tissues. And a lot of space. Yet surprisingly, it is not lonely.

There are sessions with Grace. And in-between these meetings there are steps. These steps are to be taken at my speed.

According to Grace, the role of a coach is to encourage and remind, and ask some tough questions. You know, call me on my shit.

She explained to me that, once I understood how the brain works, in terms of how it creates artificial happiness, I'd be on my way to giving the brain some oxygen. She offered the word 'movement' instead of exercise (it felt better, really it did) and said that, whatever I wanted to call it, exercise/movement is a great way to shift thought patterns.

Apparently, the results of intentionally moving around set the stage for success in all the other habits. Grace shares, with all those who are open to learning, that movement stirs up all kinds of good-stuff inside the body and starts the base of a happy soup of chemicals (nothing artificial). Basically, those who move think more clearly, learn quicker, and appreciate deeper.

Coaches must get sick of clients confusing life changes with weight change.

"Jane," Grace said, "losing weight doesn't guarantee happiness. And neither does building a six pack. Happiness is produced from a combination of practices—call them habits—and those habits decorate the whole-body-mind-soul in abundance of inner-happiness."

But exercise and discipline meant evil (to me), and I don't do evil.

A few weeks ago, I never would have thought that 'moving my body around' was the first thing I ought to do—I had such a shitty track record with gyms and team sports. Why couldn't we start with a spa day?

For a long time, I'd felt that, if I could just get rid of the extra thirty-five pounds I was carrying around, I'd fly through the house with super-cleaning power, I'd land an interview with a firm (drop forty pounds and I'd start my own consulting business), and Jack would want to hold my hand like he'd done before the kids were born. I wanted to believe that I just hadn't found the right 'diet'.

But in the last six months, what had brought me to Grace was knowing that losing ten, twenty, thirty, or even forty pounds had as much chance of changing my life as a herd of golden horned unicorns appearing in the field behind our house.

Even though Grace told me there was nothing wrong with me, when she said 'movement' and 'discipline' I saw a massive learning curve—a steep hill—to happiness.

My legs had started to cramp already and my stomach grumbled; yet, the idea of inner-happiness—such seductive words—and having an entire landscape around me that was not fraught with chaos, was interesting enough to make me stay through the appointment.

I knew there was no instant fix, but I wanted one nonetheless. I wanted a fun life. But when had it last felt like fun? The fun only lasted for short-term, during numb-outs: a box of chocolates, a bag of chips, or a tub of ice cream could do that. So could a couple of glasses of red wine, and an eleven at night to three in the morning Netflix binge. Instant joy, all of it.

I was imagining a cherry-brandy filled dark treat when Grace asked, "What are the odds of you dying right now?"

Shocked the hell out of me.

"What about tomorrow? What are the odds you'll drop dead tomorrow?"

I remained speechless. I didn't like to think about that. What I did like was to drive through Timmies, pick up a half dozen Boston Creams, and save them until everyone was sleeping. The staleness was worth it; the proven way to get me through the day so I could cope with the evening routine of stay-at-home mom-dom, punctuated by a husband working late or out of town. Four Boston Creams—did I forget to mention that two were consumed in the afternoon?—gobbled down while I let my dreams of a career fade into the credits of a child's movie left running in the family room.

Fortunately, Grace picked up on my discomfort—I suppose she'd seen this reaction before.

She explained how 'marketing' of all things—sophisticated, subliminal, money-grabbing schemes—had come up with slogans to support my desire for instant gratification.

- Get a loan and buy whatever you want now.
- Eat whatever you want because today may be your last day.
- Thirty days to a new you. Guaranteed. Operators are standing by.
- Health issues ten years from now? We'll have a cure.

The superficiality of now. The immediate solution. The big easy.

Mentally, I identified with them all, and added a pinch of: *zone out and escape reality because reality sucks for you... true, wonderful reality belongs to slender, self-employed, entrepreneurial women with university degrees and six-figure contracts.*

She re-reassured me again by saying there was nothing wrong with me. It was like she read my freaking mind.

I'm glad Grace read my mind because when it came down to it, I truly believed I was a loser and was at fault for being overweight, out of shape, and having a bit of a temper. I had some strong beliefs that I would never amount to anything. They had grown as the years passed, as the pounds went on, since I'd had more acne, and more than what I considered an average number of sore throats and colds. I carried my so-called faults with me at all times, and labeled myself damaged, ready to break.

The days when I saw others happy and succeeding in healthy ways, I harboured resentment. And sometimes, when the kids spent a weekend at their grandparents, I'd decide I was broken, stay in bed for hours, then glue myself back together minutes before their return.

Who knew 'advertising, skewed societal norms, money-hungry profiteers with instant fixes for problems by way of plying marketing strategies and messing with minds', was hooking up with the part of my brain that was easy prey?

I waited for Grace to say, "Just fooling, Jane. Sign here. Write a cheque, and I guarantee you, a money back warrantee, that in five weeks you'll be everything you want to be and more." A crazy fantasy, since I still had the brain cells to know that in order to reach any goal it takes time—in order to graduate I'd had to go to kindergarten, elementary, junior high, and high school, where, year after year, I'd attended classes, read books, and taken tests. I'd put in the time.

Oh, shit, was it going to take thirteen years, like school? The kids would be adults then.

There was nothing wrong with me.
It would not take thirteen years.
It would not take thirteen minutes, either.
There was nothing wrong with me.

And the discipline. I swore to myself, if she said struggle and discipline one more time, I'd fake sick and leave—but I knew that was a lie too. I trusted her. It felt right being with her. She was more honest with me than I had been with me.

Discipline may have sounded like going to the office and getting the strap. A mean old witch with a wooden spoon. A grumpy old geezer of a principal with a switch. An authoritarian with a yardstick. But that was before I looked at 'discipline' as a form of self-leadership, an inner higher-self to follow, an ultimate investment advisor within myself.

Collateral Happiness: The Power Behind the Facade

I was warming up to the new definition when she dropped the L-bomb.

Grace said that I was worthy and deserving of happiness. She said that one day I would say the words, 'I LOVE myself.'

In that moment I so wanted to believe her.

I wondered how many times she said, 'there is nothing wrong with you' to her other clients. I was probably some extraordinary case; inside, I thought she might be rolling her eyes.

"I love you?" That's what perfect parents say to children who sleep like angels.

"I love you?" That's what soulmates croon to each other in the last moments of wakefulness.

And it was then that I extracted my first tissue from her 'value size' box.

"I love you?" Those three words scared the living shit out of me.

I watched Grace through tears. She wasn't rolling her eyes. She wasn't Ms. Judge-ey McPrejudice Pants. She was compassionate, direct, and empathetic.

She asked me, when I breathed in and out, if I 'sort of breathed' or did I commit to breathing one-hundred percent, since anything less would cause my death?

Well that was a no brainer. Of course I breathed one-hundred percent.

And I started to see what she was getting at. Commitment. Investment in self. Guidance from a coach. Not pity. Guidance. Empathy.

I pictured those first-grade readers our grandparents would have used. *Dick and Jane.*

'"Run Jane, Run." I hadn't realized I'd said it out loud.

"You've got this," said Grace.

"I'm not so sure yet." I thought about the times when I'd woken with the worst food hangovers and had no energy or motivation to do anything. I was living to exist, but I wasn't really living intentionally in my purpose. Purpose? When had I last considered I had a purpose? I was almost 40. Was it even possible or worth it to figure it out now?

"Jane, there's this story from the *Eat, Pray, Love* film: A joke about a poor man who goes to church every day and prays before the statue of a great saint: 'Dear saint, please, please, please… give me the grace to win the lottery.' This lament goes on for months. Finally the exasperated statue comes to life, looks down at the begging man and says in weary disgust, 'My son, please, please, please… buy a ticket.' Jane, you can't just wish for happiness and expect it to fall in your lap. At some point you'll have to 'buy the ticket'. That translates to doing the work of learning and putting that learning into action."

"This is gonna hurt, isn't it?" I asked.

"Yes, but I'll be right here alongside. You won't be going it alone," she answered. "And, after a time, you'll find you're right alongside yourself."

'How much is it gonna hurt?' I asked.

"Depends. Everyone moves at his or her own pace."

For a moment I wished I'd cancelled the meeting. For a nano-second I grieved the upcoming loss of what I was about to lose—my old self, the person I was used to. Awful as I was, I was the only me I had, the only me I knew. I would miss the familiarity of feeling fat, out of shape, without purpose. After all, what would I say to myself in all those empty moments when I usually complained or made nasty comments about myself to myself? Who would eat the Boston Creams?

I closed my eyes and watched a transformed Jane floating. The landscape below looked peaceful. I didn't see Mary, ever the pessimist, peeking out her living room window. Instead, I saw flower beds, and smiling people including me; islands of fun all over the neighbourhood. And when the 'on the earth me' looked up at 'the floating me', I... she... noticed the sun was shining. I saw the floor plan in my home, as if the roof was off. My kitchen was clean. My bed was made. The kids' beds were made. And surprise of all surprises, the spare bedroom had been made into an office.

"Are you feeling alright?" Grace asked. "Do you need some water?"

"Um, yeah, sure. I'm okay. It's just that I saw a kind of snapshot."

"And how did it look?"

I smiled. "Like I had opened a happiness bank account and was getting a phenomenal return on investment."

"That sounds promising," she said.

"What next?" I asked.

She shot back a question, "One hundred percent committed?"

And the word came out of my mouth before I could stop it. "Absolutely."

"You might hate me at times," she said.

"I can live with that," I said. "I just don't want to hate myself anymore."

"So next, we're gonna move, then we're going to eat well, and we're going to begin to learn about rest and relaxation. Are you ready?"

"I'm ready." I replied.

"Discipline is really freedom," said Grace.

A warm wave came over me; apparently it didn't show on my face.

"When I had self-doubt, it really helped me to remember that thoughts we think over and over turn into beliefs." said Grace.

"You had self-doubts?"

"Jane, I once ordered a large pizza and a full Chinese takeout dinner. Ate it in one sitting, then went outside because the food sweats were so bad."

And for the first time in absolutely ages, I laughed. A real laugh. "So I guess I'll get moving; maybe walking," I said.

"Baby steps," she said. "It's the small steps that are going to help you create that place of happiness. And I'm really looking forward to going on this journey of change with you."

"Well, I guess unless I change who I am I'll always be who I am now." One hour and I'd become a philosopher.

"That's what I always say too," replied Grace.

The Approach and Formula for the Creation of Collateral Happiness

Step one and two were heavy. Perhaps new material. Most programs dive right into food and calories (with a sale's pitch).

In the 'Dear Reader', you were asked to hold this book to your heart and introduce yourself to it. That's because I want you to imagine me on paper, as if I, Christine the human, shapeshifted into a book.

So, at a first meeting I would ask you:

1. What is your intention in meeting with me as a coach?
2. What do you want to achieve?
3. What are you needing from me?

Then I would share my intentions as an example to help you form your own.

My intentions as your coach are to: influence, inspire, recommend, guide, educate and motivate you. To hold you accountable. To be your biggest support, fan, and cheerleader. To hold zero judgement of you whatsoever. And to create a safe, confidential, loving space for you to be vulnerable and grow.

I cannot make the changes and do the work for you.

I can only steer you. I can only provide the means and information, but it is up to you to do with it what you wish. You are responsible for your success.

So how can people create change required for growth?

Approach and Formula for the Creation of Collateral Happiness

Unless we change how we are, we will always have what we've got. We create change by adapting and honoring our actions with the science and psychology of humans, rather than working against it. We must:

1. find an inspiration that pulls us toward a goal, or a desperation which compels us to abandon suffering;
2. establish and repeat positive habits (which is why this is not an overnight process);
3. change our influences (which is why we cannot speak it into existence alone);
4. get used to feeling discomfort (leaning into it rather than avoiding it);
5. set up accountability; just like when we lived with our parents who told us to do things which we did not like to do, we are not going to like to do new things initially because it is our natural reaction;
6. let go of past experiences, assumptions and conclusions (our past does not predict our future);
7. take small steps (our brain can better handle this as opposed to giant leaps);
8. apply the laws of human nature in order to attain real collateral happiness, otherwise we spend our time looking for short bursts of artificial pleasure.

Change without progress is just movement.

When positive changes are made, and those changes improve or solve a problem, people often stop taking the actions that caused the 'problem' to improve. They think the problem is over, but it's not. It doesn't mean the problem went away and was solved forever. It's a matter of cause and effect. To maintain the solution, the changes and habits that were implemented to attain the desired outcome will forever need to be followed.

For example: after you've reached a weight loss goal, it doesn't mean the problem went away and the weight will stay off if you get to go back to old ways. To maintain the weight loss, you have to follow, long-term, what it was that helped you reach the weight loss goal. If you don't, the original challenges are still there and the weight comes back on. That's why it is critical to find a solution for change that can forever be implemented, not just a temporary one. If not, the problem will continually keep resurfacing.

Just because we create more change does not mean we receive more out of life. Change is not just about having adventure and variety. It also needs to build upon itself. In order to create collateral happiness we can approach change in a way that allows us to learn, progress and adjust.

When we are in a place of genuine happiness, it is much easier to sustain long-lasting results.

Another thing I do when I meet with a client is inform them that I will call them out on his or her BS. Why? I am here to help each person push limits and boundaries. I am here to stop the negative stories and excuses they tell themselves. In order for each individual to reach goals, each person will be required to do things not done before, which requires a step, or two, or three outside each person's comfort zone.

In being each person's biggest fan, loudest cheerleader, and strongest support, I will always be here. I'll ask each person to use a journal to have rants about me and about the process—use those rants as your shouting into pillow moments; in fact, shout into pillows. Then hold the book close to your heart and continue the work.

A journal is where people can let it all out and not hold back or worry. There is nothing anyone could do that I would see as unfit. I respect, and hold in high regard, every individual who wants to improve. I see courage and strength and inspiration. There are no such things as failures; only lessons.

To fail is actually to learn. To call yourself a failure is to call yourself a student.

For those who don't meet a commitment for some reason, please do not avoid me (meaning please don't keep this book closed). This process is about identifying blocks and helping people get past them; if a participant doesn't show up, we cannot do that. Think of the place(s) where you read this book—the car, a coffee shop, your living room—as safe locations. Wherever you are, when this book is near, you are in a safe place, a 'working on you' space.

Creating Happiness to Live Lighter (under the umbrella of happiness in its ebbs and flows) will take a massive commitment from each person. Each of you already knows that, which is likely why you are holding this book and deeply wanting it to be the last thing to 'try' in order to be happy.

These steps are absolutely doable. This book does not so much represent a program, as it does a reprogram or reset—a way of life, reached through series of steps. A slow and steady journey. Do not race through it. This is about self-creation as opposed to self-help.

What is the goal?
True inner-happiness.

Why are we doing this?
To align with our true higher self. To alleviate shame, pain, embarrassment we feel about our lifestyle and choices. **To finally speak these words,**

> **I love myself. I am worthy. I deserve to feel happy.**

And to believe it when you speak it.

What will commitment and hard work result in?
The creation of true inner-happiness: a state of internal happiness that generates joy from within (rather than through artificial means), will lead to a stronger immune

Collateral Happiness: The Power Behind the Facade

system, a balanced and healthy weight, increased creativity, healthier relationships with others, and a sense of inner peace at the core of self.

Collateral happiness is the golden ticket we all seek in life. We need to do the work to earn the money to buy the ticket, then go out and purchase the ticket, and finally attend a grand event with each one of us at centre stage.

THE CHART/FORMULA FOR COLLATERAL HAPPINESS

Negative Life Path
External-Based Happiness

Negative Habits
Inactivity, Poor Nutrition, Distractions, Lack of Knowledge, Isolation or Negative Relationship, Ungrateful

+

Self-Unawareness
Zone Out, Avoid, Apathetic, Lack of Meaning

+

Self-Hatred

+

Artificial "Fix"
Binge Eating, Addiction. Put on a Facade, Live in Fear

=

Artificial Happiness

Positive Life Path
Internal-Based Happiness

Positive Habits
Movement, Good Nutrition, Spiritual Practice, Learning, Positive Relationships, Mindfulness

+

Self-Awareness
Goals and Commitments, Passion and Purpose, Scheduling and Priorities, Values, Overcoming Self-Limiting Beliefs, Pain and Pleasure, Metaprograms, Changing Language, Positive Influences

+

Self Love
6 Core Human Needs, Forgiveness and Acceptance

+

Authenticity
Facing Our Fears, Stepping Outside Our Comfort Zone

=

Collateral Happiness

Energy must flow as it is not static. When it comes to creating happiness, there is a choice of a negative or positive flow of energy. It is up to each individual to choose which path to direct energy—to choose artificial happiness or collateral happiness.

Step Three:
The Basics on the Laws of Spirit (Human Nature)

WHY DO WE NEED TO UNDERSTAND THE LAWS OF HUMAN NATURE?

We are spiritual beings having a human experience, yet very few of us have learned the Universal Laws, as some call laws of nature or spirit. I refer to them as Laws of Human Nature. Knowledge of these laws has an effect upon mental impulses which allows us to attain mental clarity about who we are as humans. The Laws give us a better understanding about how to live in harmony and flow. They help steer our human psyche to make order within chaos; to approach pain with less struggle.

When we align our lives—positive habits, self-awareness, self-love, and authenticity—to the laws of human nature, we can bring meaning to our struggles and create collateral happiness. We can stop resisting what is inherent to our being, and start to honor what makes us human. We can stop feeling bad about ourselves for 'not getting it right'.

We will have a tendency to want to skip the understanding of these laws; we may not want to hear them, and/or may be bored by them, but without the foundational understanding of the laws of human nature—the laws which govern the forces of nature—we will endure struggle, even experience mental anguish, when we defy them.

To live as a human in harmony within nature is to exist as a learner; not always to be flawless.

> Human laws form a basis of social agreement and social order, but human laws are only a pale reflection of a higher order of laws sewn into the fabric of existence. These laws govern the movement of the earth, cycle of the seasons, the forces of nature, and the structure of the atom itself. Nature didn't make these laws; nature only reveals and demonstrates them. The great laws existed before humanity, before nature.
>
> Dan Millman, *The Life You Were Born to Live*

LAW OF DISCIPLINE

We live in a society that accepts instant gratification as a guiding belief, which defies the law of discipline. Here's the thing... we cannot change a law. We can only change our beliefs about the law. This law signifies a paradox in that we achieve freedom through discipline.

Through discipline we are able to achieve depth of skill, knowledge, and fluency which allows us increased options—freedom and independence.

Freedom is the result of discipline, not its absence. On the outside, it appears that freedom is an esteemed avoidance of boundaries and limitations—free of the ball and chain; do anything, anytime, anywhere. An abundance of freedom, upfront, sacrifices achievement of skill and proficiency down the road.

Applying rigorous habits assumes greater burden. With it comes greater freedom. Economic responsibility brings freedom to spend money. Nurturing the body with exercise and a suitable diet results in a gain of physical power; everything becomes a trade-off with cause and effect.

Many people never advance because they are unwilling to bring rigor to their life. Things are put off until tomorrow. Excessive materialism over-extends limits on resources and time.

Those who are happy and successful bring their body, emotions, and mind into perfect control. Discipline and commitment applied daily becomes the bridge between now and achieved goals. The key is to find a goal that is inspirational enough to justify the adversity of discipline.

Example: 4 years of university is not 'all' fun and doesn't 'always' feel good, however, through the discipline, we attain a degree which gives us knowledge, and provides a type of freedom by expanding our career options.

LAW OF FLEXIBILITY

This law is about embracing and being aware of the present moment: viewing problems as opportunities and having the strength to bend and flex with what comes our way rather than being rigid in our expectations. Just like a tree when it is unable to bend, it breaks.

It is the acceptance of what we cannot change within our current circumstances.

To be flexible is to be responsive with 'in the moment' occurrences rather than resisting, fighting or denying the truth of the situation. When we are of fixed mindset, unwilling to bend and accept that things did not go as planned, we feel the moment as pain rather than as what it is meant to be, which is merely a call to action—an opportunity to each realign to our higher self.

> Our bodies, when free of external programming and interference, abide naturally within these laws, which are communicated through our instincts and subtle intuitive feelings. All we have to do is pay attention to and trust our inner knower. The mind or ego, our isolated sense of separate self, resists the flow of the current of life.
>
> Dan Millman, *The Life You Were Born to Live*

LAW OF CHOICES

Humans have the free will to express their creative energies in positive or negative ways.

Awareness of beliefs enhances the ability to choose. Many mind-sets ascribe to the idea that 'Life sorta happens to us'. This is true if we fail to choose.

Within every situation we have the power and ability to choose how to respond.

At times we may feel that our 'hands are tied', but we always have a choice; we just may not like the consequences. Since it is our survival instinct to avoid pain, we may feel limited in our choice due to unacceptance of undesirable consequences. Our power of choice exponentially increases the fewer the limiting beliefs we hold. It is each individual's prerogative to choose their path, whether it be easy or difficult, with each decision followed by a consequence.

LAW OF RESPONSIBILITY

The ability to respond as a conscious choice.

Each individual is wise to take responsible action for his or her own emotional, physical, mental, and spiritual well-being.

We are responsible for our own feelings and cannot protect others from their own. We are here to help others only within the boundaries that we set for ourselves. It is our responsibility to establish personal boundaries of what we are willing and not willing to do. If we base our self-worth on our ability to serve others and protect their feelings, we lead ourselves to become enslaved to that obligation.

It's essential for each of us to take full responsibility for our own life while not blaming, criticizing or projecting negative feelings onto others. To blame others is to give up our power and responsibility for our own course of action.

We are all responsible for our success in life. We cannot assume others will do it for us.

LAW OF BALANCE

In life there exists an ebb and flow of opposites to which each individual is to pay attention, and keep in balance. To achieve balance is to achieve peace and fulfillment.

We can explore extreme polarities as we move through life. The goal is to seek balance, over time, in the center—the fulcrum.

Mistakes and failures that we experience from exploring extremes and testing limits help us learn where each of our balance points rests. Since the balance point is different for each person, most would rather 'test the waters' than take advice from other sources. This increased participation in trial may cause greater tribulation; this experience we call life creates joy for us when we participate within our own awareness, not someone else's.

Places we may see this law applied can be noted with such things as give and take, pain and pleasure, masculine and feminine, negative and positive, full and empty, losses and gains. Each one pulls us back and forth in a natural rhythmical pattern to find our center. Each extreme is neither good nor bad, just the flow and rhythm of life.

Rather than arrange a deck of cards by lining up the outside edges, line them up by stringing a hole in each card so that you can see right through the deck.

LAW OF ACTION

Action—not always an easy law to follow—is putting all the thoughts, beliefs, intentions into motion, and turning them into results; challenging because the forces of doubt and inertia exist within our mind and body. It's essential to overcome insecurity and self-doubt, lethargy, apathy, and excuses, in order to stay the course.

Regardless of what dreams, goals, aspirations, we think or feel, it is only action which brings them into reality. Act on them despite uncertainty.

There is never a time that is perfect—feels good or right. Just do it as '5-4-3-2-1-go'.

Any time we take a risk to follow intention with action, we are met by a sense of satisfaction.

LAW OF NO JUDGEMENT

Judgement is a man-made illusion as the universe does not judge. It merely provides opportunity to redirect course.

Using comparison (to our own ideals) as a standard of measurement is unfair, flawed, and sets us up for failure. We live in a real world with real people who grow, learn, fail, make mistakes, and evolve uniquely and individually.

Setting ideals close to perfection incurs a greater stress to prove and improve ourselves, fearful of being inadequate against our own standards. Ironically, those of us with the highest standards may have the lowest self-worth because we feel we are never good enough.

It is important to practice infinite non-judgement in order to experience, learn, heal, grow and evolve. If we stop judging our own self, we will perceive less judgement directed at us by others.

LAW OF PROCESS

In order to accomplish anything in life, it is necessary to follow—with patience—a gradual process. It is much easier to achieve a small step than a giant leap.

This law teaches us not only to break a journey into shorter sections but also to appreciate and celebrate each step as if it were an end in itself. Life becomes more joyous when we value the journey more than the emphasis we place on the destination.

LAW OF PATTERNS

When we were young we learned to make sense of the world by observing patterns as part of our mechanism of survival. We developed complex associations of meaning through these repeated patterns.

Any pattern, whether identified as good or bad, will reassert itself over time unless we break that pattern by doing something different.

Habit patterns of pleasure can be reinforced with self reward.

Habit patterns of pain—dysfunctional, negative, or destructive—require full acknowledgment as the first step to interruption of that old pattern.

Stating 'it is going to be different this time' or 'I won't do it again' isn't enough.

Old patterns will reassert unless broken by doing something different rather than remaining a victim by repeating them.

Insanity is doing the same thing and expecting different results.

There are many more 'laws' of human nature. These nine are significant to the changes we can make to create collateral happiness.

PART III
HABITS OF COLLATERAL HAPPINESS

Movement
Nutrition
Spiritual Practice
Creativity/Learning
Positive Relationships
Mindfulness

Step Four:
Appreciating the Habits

Ninety-five percent of everything we do is the result of habit. Habit is our subconscious mind at work.

This means that 95% of how we think and what we do is driven by the subconscious mind. So if we want to create happiness and success, we will have a much better chance if we form habits that create that happiness and success, rather than only relying on conscious thoughts.

How do we form habits? Through repetition. We cannot just speak a habit into existence, so we have to retrain the mind to move a thought from conscious to subconscious by repeating it consistently over time. We must also choose to release the negative subconscious belief that conflicts with the new positive habit.

It takes skill to create habits and, "skill is myelin insulation that wraps neural circuits and that grows according to certain signals," states Daniel Coyle in the book, *The Talent Code*. Myelin Theory as described in *The Talent Code* explains that, in order to develop skill, we do so through deep practice:

> (1) Every human movement, thought or feeling is a precisely timed electric signal travelling through a chain of neurons —a circuit of nerve fibers. (2) Myelin is the insulation that wraps these nerve fibers and increases signal strength, speed, and accuracy. (3) The more we fire a particular circuit, the more myelin optimizes that circuit, and the stronger, faster, and more fluent our movements and thoughts become.

This means repetition; practice and be patient in developing the skill to create habits, because the more we do it the more fluent our thoughts and actions become.

It works the same in reverse. Negative habits cannot just be broken overnight, but they can be replaced by a new positive habit through repetitive action.

When we want to grow or change, we typically get a conscious thought about it and then basically a battle between the subconscious and conscious mind ensues. The subconscious mind sends the body signals of discomfort when it senses danger (whether that danger is physical (falling off a building) or is emotional (public speaking for the first time) because the body is designed for survival).

When we sense physical or emotional danger, the mind responds by signaling the body to get away from the threat.

In order to grow and thrive (change habits, introduce new behaviours), we need to understand the biological response and overcome running away.

Using the conscious part of the brain 'hurts'. Think mental marathon. Once a habit is subconscious it becomes easy, and prevents a battle of the minds every time we perform the habit.

This is why growth and change for the positive is so difficult. It's not because there is anything wrong with us, it is because we don't understand the biology and psychology of the body and mind.

When we want to grow and change we must:

1. learn to resist the inherent biological pull of the subconscious mind that is designed to keep us comfortable and safe for our survival—embrace discomfort as part of growth;

2. retrain the brain through consistent repetition in order to create habits, which are driven, eventually, by the subconscious mind because the subconscious mind drives the majority of what we do.

The process of creating a new habit or belief—taking a conscious thought and making it subconscious—is what I call moving through surviving to thriving. The process of retraining the brain and creating habits is difficult, takes time, requires conscious energy, and feels unnatural.

If we don't' care for change or growth we are not failures; we simply need to understand the biology and psychology of the mind, and know how it works, in order to overcome the fear of change. When we understand this process, we can stop beating ourselves up and start taking approaches to change which follow the mind's natural functioning.

Developing positive habits in order to reach inner-happiness can be compared to how teeth-brushing is almost a subconscious practice.

Did you brush your teeth... yet?

How many times did you hear this as a child or say it as a parent?

Those reminders became the 'not thinking about it but doing it because it would be strange not to do it'.

It's doubtful that your parents enforced 'habits of happiness' the same way they pushed for dental hygiene.

- Did your parent(s) make you exercise each day? If not, exercise is unlikely a habit in your lifestyle.

- Did anyone make you meditate each day? If not, you probably don't use meditation as a daily requirement for restoration of your body, mind, and soul.

- Did someone significant instill in your 'behaviour' that reading every day was a normal activity? If not, then daily reading might feel extremely foreign to you, even difficult.

- Did a caregiver make you take two tablespoons of chia seeds every day? If not, it's unlikely you open wide and force yourself, once a day, to endure a few seconds of displeasure and take a spoon of chia seeds for extra fibre.

The point is that some things are not fun, nor do we like to do them, but they are still good for us—we reap the benefits later. We develop habits so the things that create inner-happiness become a normal part of our day without having to consciously force ourselves to do it. We do it because it becomes our routine.

Sometimes we may need a parent or a coach or a boss to hold us accountable and to be persistent with us in order to retrain the mind and ingrain new habits. We may even despise them for doing this. The important thing to note is that we recognize how we best need to be pushed through that sweet spot between the inherent instincts of surviving to thriving.

As adults, there may still be times when we need a 'parent' figure to help us create new positive habits—example: coach or personal trainer. We may despise them for making us do something we hate, but we can also love them for the same reason. They force us to do the things we don't want to do, but know those things will be good for us. That is why investing in someone who can help keep you accountable is a good thing and does not mean there is anything wrong with you. Yes, we all know we 'should' do it, but sometimes we need someone to help us stay committed to doing it. And that is okay. It is completely human.

We are still like young kids resisting new tasks that are viewed as a chore. We know these chores are necessary for a happy and healthy existence, but as adults we don't have anyone forcing us to ensure that we do them, so we choose not to.

Avoiding incorporating these habits of happiness is like going for days without teeth-brushing or showering.

It also goes the other way round. If you want to change patterns in your kids or your employees, understand that initially there may be resistance. They may despise you. It is our natural instinct, even if we know the result will be good for us. You may have to remind them to do something constantly, but rather than get mad or frustrated, understand that retraining the mind takes time. The process goes much better when it can be associated with a positive experience as opposed to a negative one. No matter our age, we need time to retrain the mind. We are all human. Learning to be patient with ourselves and with others is key.

All habits can be learned or replaced through repetition. That is why small, boring habits implemented daily create happiness. There is no one giant leap that does it. It's a lot of little 'unsexy' steps compounded. No, it's not easy, but it is worth it.

Conversely, we have also formed habits that are not good for us, that destroy our bodies and affect our brain capacity, but, because we do these things regularly, almost without thinking, the consequences of those habits (which often generate temporary/artificial happiness) are devastating. If you cannot accept the logic of habit and discipline (investing in the self), you will lose out on healthy and happy because habits are necessary in order to make it happen.

For example, if a person has a belief that she is not attractive, hearing the compliment once will cause her to feel good in the moment, but won't have a lasting impact. For that person to believe she is attractive, she will need to develop a habitual response of positive self-image. She will require to override her programmed negative thoughts.

When it comes to retraining the mind, we may have setbacks during the process of creating a new habit. This is normal. If we know we need to eat healthily, but one day find ourselves mindlessly grabbing unhealthy food, we don't need to get angry at ourselves. We need to be aware that retraining the brain is a process and not just a decision.

Be patient with this approach of applying new habits of success. Remember it took a while before we brushed our teeth without being told or reminded.

Research suggests it takes about 60ish days of repetition to create a habit. That's an average; none of us are numbers. It's not a race. We can simply move through each day with our eye on our desires: healthy body, mind, soul. We can remind ourselves that the beauty of creating a habit is that it becomes an unconscious, ingrained activity which frees us from consciously having to make ourselves do something.

Ultimately, it is not how much materialism we possess that is most important. It is how well we actively participate in our own life.

Habit #1: Movement

Before we open our mouths to eat and drink, we breathe. And so it makes sense that before we do anything, we inhale and exhale. Breathing fuels the body with oxygen.

When we focus on movement, exercise, working-out—whatever you wish to call it—we naturally release happy hormones which put us in a state to be more positive, and with that we can find clarity. If we want to address our mental state of mind and create happiness, it means we need to address the physical body so it does not interfere and conflict with the mind.

For example, if we sit on the couch and eat fast food every day, we know that we won't feel good—in fact, it will disrupt our neurotransmitters. We won't just feel bad physically, we will feel bad mentally.

Being in a better state of mind and body makes it much easier to tackle difficult things down the road, like facing our fears or talking about issues from the past. If we were only to address the mental issues, but kept abusing or neglecting our body, it would counteract the results. We would limit our progress. **We cannot have a positive state of mind without having a positive state of body.** A balanced body, mind, and spirit is necessary in order to create collateral happiness.

Movement is emphasized because it is more than a means to lose weight, look thin, or get fit. We don't 'have to' go to the gym to be successful or popular. If we only see exercise in this light, and we happen not to care about what we look like, then it gives us an excuse not to do it.

Movement accomplishes so much more beyond physical.

There's a requirement, in moving toward collateral happiness, to lighten up on our definition of 'exercise'. Exercise can be something completely different to each one of us. It might be going to the gym. It might be going for a walk. It might be dancing naked in our room. It might take 15 minutes. It might take 30 minutes, or 60. We might have physical limitations. The key is to move within our means.

The point is that to do what is right for us as individuals and not what everyone else is doing or telling us to do. From this point on, exercise will be replaced by 'movement'. Please take some time to define movement in your own mind's eye.

Movement helps us to feel naturally happy by releasing endorphins. When we move we decompress. Simply moving the body takes us in the direction of feeling happier.

Well what about moving for the physical body?—as in workouts and physical fitness. Of course, we need to move in order to maintain physical health and to overcome challenge or injury, or prevent illness or injury. The point is, movement is more than shaping the body; it shapes the mind.

Movement 'first' is paramount for the rest of the steps in creating inner-happiness. Yes, the other steps are important, and will flow together (nutrition, meditation, relationships, rest and relaxation, self-awareness, learning), but doesn't it makes sense to get the brain in its optimum mode for receiving all that is to come? All those 'deposits' as 'Jane' might call them. Those investments in self.

When the blood is flowing and the heart is happy to be beating, we can more easily focus on the other aspects of creating inner-happiness.

For various reasons, it is common to want to put exercise last, even when we have a handle on everything else. "We never liked

Habit #1: Movement

exercise." "We don't have time." "We can't afford to go to the gym." "We have a bad back."

Wanting to wait and put exercise until last is a mistake.

There is no better way to start the journey to true inner-happiness than with a brain ready to receive healthy information. Therefore, we get our heart pumping and we move oxygen to the brain.

There's no request to join a gym here, or to buy any expensive equipment, but please do if you so wish. The first movements to include are things that we like. Maybe its music—some of us play a great air guitar—some of the biggest rock stars are super-fit and have amazing stamina to stay on stage. So, turn up the speakers and do whatever you need to do to move to the music. Dance classes are completely optional.

For those who are quite orderly and have a hard time identifying what would be enjoyable, take whatever device you have and stream some free workouts; there is everything from walking to yoga available for every level. Available with one click.

Worrying already how it will all fit into your life? Overthinking what seems like a tall order? Stop. One step at a time. There is a great deal of time squandered on wallowing, procrastinating in all of our pasts. It has taken up chunks of energy in various forms of avoidance.

Logistics click into place when we move our bodies. I'm not asking you to run a marathon or even walk a kilometre. Just start with what you can manage, and commit to it.

Most people's days are already filled with travel time, personal hygiene, administrative tasks (paying bills, for example), and work. To truly experience success and inner-happiness, creating time for moving has to become a priority—a daily part of life—not just something we do sporadically when we 'have time' or 'feel like it'.

Collateral Happiness: The Power Behind the Facade

It's time to start shifting paradigms about body, mind, and spirit existing as separate entities. These three aspects of our being are intertwined. It's necessary to move away from the kind of thinking that we only exercise and eat healthy for our body and that we only meditate for our mind and spirit. Total acknowledgement of being one connected being is prerequisite to creating inner-happiness. (I will introduce them separately so as not to overwhelm.)

Prior to beginning any kind of movement, it's great, in the spirit of knowing that it is an all in—body, mind, soul—to ask an important question: "Am I happy?"

Do not confuse the question with: "Am I in great shape? Am I too fat or too thin?"

Focusing on weight and fitness level is a disastrous distraction; the ultimate procrastination—a direct route to total avoidance so as not to have to ask and answer a question equally important to the one about happiness: Who am I?

Movement naturally releases happy hormones. For free. No prescription.

Call it exercise, movement, active living, participation, or activity. Label it dancing, skipping, hopping, walking, hiking. Use the word that fits for you and doesn't turn you off. Make up a new one. Christine-ing, Growing, Stretching, Susan-ing, Karen-ing. But do not call it anything that evokes negative feelings.

If you were the last one chosen for sports in school, or got a note to skip sports day, then honour those feelings of rejection and participate in your personal version of movement.

That means finding something you enjoy.

Movement is useful for more than just losing weight and looking fit. That is why it's a good idea no longer to relate to movement for those reasons. Instead, focus on moving for 'whole-body' reasons as opposed to only physical body.

Habit #1: Movement

The benefits associated with a movement routine: (not one of the benefits mentions reduction of calories)

- Allows the release and flow of creative energy. Seriously, ask any successful creative.
- Creates a higher vibrational frequency to support healing.
- Assists the body to build strength and stamina, both of which are necessary for staying productive.
- **Provides a path to clear thinking and promotes overall positive attitude which makes each of us a better 'coach' 'manager' 'cook' 'admin assistant' 'nurse'... (insert any career or role here).**
- Releases happy hormones into the body, such as endorphins, without the need for food to boost the brain.
- Generates physical and emotional energy which changes mental state from negative to positive meaning, and results in better decision making.

The more we move, the more ways we find we want to incorporate it. People who begin with one song a day (dancing and playing air guitar) soon find themselves wanting to add another and another until they are 'performing' physical routines and loving them. In addition, this increased fitness level leads to these same people making the choice to walk to the store or take the stairs, just for the great feeling that movement delivers.

Within a short time, moving people discover that the resulting healthy mind, benefiting from happy hormones, has provided more room to think out the solutions to a work situation or formulate how to handle a family issue, a business problem, or an internal dilemma.

Client Focus I

Female, forty-something, told as child no rhythm, hated gym at school.

Appreciate that someone who rarely moved around now dances in her bedroom each morning. What began with one song is now a stretching session, an aerobic and strength building party for one. By the time she gets in the shower—only steps away from where she dances—her mind is clear. Grateful for the ability to simply move, to freely move, she finds herself singing in shower. At breakfast she feels great; all those happy hormones are turned on. The day is just beginning and she's already 'moved'.

She says if **she** can do it—and her story is fairly background-traumatic—anyone "can-can". Dancing every morning, right out of bed, holds her back none, pushes her forward in so many positive directions.

She doesn't see it as punishment. Yet, she does choose to make that commitment every morning. She knows the reward is confidence the entire day. She understands she is beginning work with happy hormones and lots of oxygen in her system. She is human. So here's what she does: When she wakes, before she thinks about pulling the covers over her head she says, aloud, 5-4-3-2-1 go, and does not give herself the option to second guess her decision to rise on one.

An interesting note: this client did not choose a playlist; she used the shuffle feature and started with one song. Each day she added another until she had three, then five, then seven. Randomly shuffled songs. Every morning. It met her needs since her immune system was compromised. She moved every morning. She let the random music stimulate her to think about the lyrics and give her specific meaning for each day. Like a horoscope, only musical and more fun to interpret.

Client Focus II

Female, mid-thirties, over-achiever, under exerciser.

The power of positive association allowed this client to change her relationship with her treadmill.

Habit #1: Movement

She dreaded exercise, so she didn't do it. But, being an over-achiever, felt terrible because she 'knew she was supposed to participate in exercise'. She viewed her treadmill as the enemy. The monster that cracked the exercise whip. And what a lot of money it had cost, too. Basically it became a piece of furniture that collected dust and held random sweaters and bags.

Then a glimmer of hope appeared. Look at me differently begged the massive, expensive machine. And so, she did. She removed the bags and sweaters, dusted off this amazing computer-adventure invention, and made a list.

The treadmill became an important component in her life that helped her move, created a fit body, built a strong immune system, cleared her mind. Treadmill became a partner, like a person—sure, she even spoke to it. Treadmill gave her the opportunity to enjoy music, a podcast, or read. It took her to places without her having to leave the house—what a time saver. And when it's forty-below, it's a walk in the park. Treadmill's location overlooked nature (through a window). What an outlook. What a partner. What a mindset change. From guilt-inducing high-priced clothes holder, to partner in growth, she and Treadmill had (and still have) an outstanding relationship. Her mind can go off in different directions and she can visualize her goals. She can walk or run. Treadmill is her friend: one which provides a positive experience for her complete being: mind, body, and spirit.

DURATION

Every person is different. Some people might not be able to walk around the block, so if they can do two sides of the square, fantastic, as long as they build on it. This (two sides) + the return = a full block.

Sessions, workouts, dances, worthy-outs, or moving for the love of oneself. Many names, one fantastic outcome.

For those who live in the country, say, on a farm, and never stop appreciating the view from the corral or barn that leads to the meadow, yet never venture out that way, then perhaps it's time to create a walk and start wearing down a path... hop, skip, and jump along the way. Kiss the sky. Let the oxygen flow.

Dog lovers may desire to volunteer and give back to the community, walk dogs for the SPCA, and incorporate volunteering with movement.

Perhaps there are folks who don't want to do this, but know it is important to follow the steps. Well, there's a way around that too. Simply find a television series, stream one show a day, and march, walk, pace to it so movement has taken place. It's like teeth-brushing. And before long it will be habitual, so much so that there will be an icky feeling inside (like when we can't brush our teeth) unless movement takes place.

Search for stuff to enjoy. Make that search fun.

FINANCIAL

When cash is tight and there is no money to spend on activities, the key is to challenge the self. There are many ways to 'move' for free. Borrow a workout DVD or download a complementary yoga class. The point is, stop finding excuses to avoid moving on. Stop trying to beat the system. And call a halt to the study of the 'get thin quick' approaches. They don't work. They don't last.

- The body needs oxygen, the heart and muscles need challenge.
- Take negative associations and make them positive ones.
- Call it whatever you want, but stay with your commitment and notice the difference over time.

With movement, one step leads to another and you will soon have moved, walked, hopped, skipped, jumped your away around a new world.

Habit #1: Movement

Breathe.

Pause.

Breathe.

If we knew how all of it would go
we could miss the pain
but we'd have to miss the dance.

You are moving. You are thinking about moving. You understand the need for movement. You've taken the first step of your dance.

You've identified your emotions, and answered questions at the end of each chapter. You've done a lot.

So, with an open mind, let's open the mouth. Let's eat.

Habit #2: Nutrition

Inner-happiness and 'feeling' the right size go hand-in-hand. Whether people are overweight, underweight, or just not eating well, the path to healthy-sizing flows naturally from creating balance in life.

Here we go again: inner-happiness is created by a number of habits, developed over time, that create true happiness and balance. Obtaining inner-happiness does not include finding your happiness fix artificially.

Eating is the one thing humans have been doing every day of their lives, yet there is so much misinformation, and myriad differences in opinion, on nutrition. How can one person's approach be better than someone else's?

We are all unique, but share the chemistry that responds to artificial stimulants. So to answer the 'approach' question: the best plan is the one we will commit to, follow, and that makes us feel our best.

And the easiest plans to commit to, when we are developing habits, is to keep it simple, natural, and eat whole food.

Eating is a choice about making it manageable and satisfying. Complicated practices and tedious routines are overwhelming and time consuming. Being mindful is important. Counting every calorie is unnecessary.

Food serves us from a calorie and nutrition perspective giving us our necessary energy, nutrients, vitamins and minerals, and food affects our vibrational energy. Healthy food carries a high vibrational energy that helps make strong bodies. Eating unhealthy food will lower vibrational energy which, in turn, will attract more of the same low energy in our life. This has been scientifically proven.

http://healthcenternutrition.webs.com/vibrationalfood.htm

- Healthy = Happy
- Seduction is the diet industry's specialty
- Marketing/ "diets" compete with authentic voice.

Beyond the clutter of artificial highs and poor habits we have developed exists a great sage, a higher self who truly understands what 'her' body requires.

- Listen to your body.
- Incorporate healthy nutrition in the same way you did with movement: one or two choices integrated a week or two at a time into your existing lifestyle; small steps based on enjoyment, balanced with the commitment to work to create a new habit.
- Begin with one approach for eating. Then incorporate another when the previous one feels natural.
- Tailor your nutrition—your everyday eating—to something that will not be short term. The most successful long-term healthy eating is reflected in a life-plan of eating a variety of delicious, healthy foods, and including a small number of foods that are old favourites.
- Give your body and brain time to recognize healthy foods, and the time to lose the response to trigger-foods that incite artificial happiness. When you do choose to eat a food that can create artificial happiness, be aware, and neither overindulge nor feel guilty. Enjoy it. When you make the time for smaller quantities of old faves, the body will not react as violently as it did in the past, when it was given those foods all the time.

It's perfectly okay to enjoy all foods that your body can tolerate well. Just not all at once.

Start living a life of clarity, by not dieting. We can't beat 'the system' by taking giant leaps. Choose one aspect for nourishing yourself and then work on incorporating a new one in a week or a month. You will eventually love yourself, and you will eventually release the weight because it's a result of truly feeling happy. You might find in a few months that you are wondering when such healthy practices became habit. But it is possible that, with small steps, simple changes (and commitment) that those habits will form. Just like the small steps in movement.

Having support is essential for accountability, and takes the pressure off that 'voice' inside you that wants this to be a quick fix. Finding the right support to help through each stage, whether it be a coach, friend, spouse, support group, nutritionist, meditation practitioner, personal trainer, or some other type of wellness practitioner, is highly recommended. Someone **who completely comprehends the priority is to discover happy and create inner-happiness.**

Small steps, solid commitment, develop habits. There is no point in going 'extreme' and eating a certain way to lose weight only to go back to old habits and regain the weight. Remember, it's not all about the food, it's about the entire realm of inner-happiness.

If you don't think you have time to encompass the entire happiness formula, consider this... **if you want something you've never had you must be willing to do something you have never done.**

If you've never been able to kick yo-yo dieting, or lose weight successfully, then accept right now that you can choose to step outside your limits and attempt something new. You will most likely feel a bit of discomfort. Remember: discomfort is the payment for collateral happiness.

Habit #2: Nutrition

PRACTICAL PRACTICE

To list some proven, effective ways to improve your eating habits and nutrition:

1. Follow the 80/20 rule to maintain a balanced mindset about eating. Choose to eat healthy, natural, unprocessed foods as 80% of your diet and enjoy the freedom to indulge as you please for the other 20%. Balanced healthy eating does not mean eating healthily 100% of the time.

2. Count gluten, dairy, soy, sugar, flour, and processed/refined food as part of the 20%. Understand this: there are no foods you cannot have. Just be sure to moderate.

3. Decide for yourself how you want to incorporate meat. It is a personal choice. Some 'bodies' do not do well without meat. Others do. The key is choosing good quality, organic meat.

4. Food combining can also be beneficial for those who experience poor digestion. Improper food combining neutralizes stomach acids which can cause inefficient digestion. For information on proper food combining check out...

Article: http://articles.mercola.com/sites/articles/archive/2013/10/27/food-combining.aspx

Chart: http://beyondhealth.com/media/wysiwyg/kadro/articles/food-Combining-chart.pdf

5. Consider looking into your nutritional type, and use 'the type' as a guide for how much protein to consume. A helpful site for determining personal nutrition types:

http://nutritionaltyping.mercola.com/Login.aspx

6. Be sure to consume enough water, daily, to aid bodily functions such as circulation, digestion, absorption of nutrients, and elimination of wastes.

7. Make it a habit to schedule your meals, even for those times you are busy.

8. Eat enough fibre. Consider chia seeds. 2-3 tablespoons a day is an adequate aim for most, but start with less so as not to

shock your system. Dr. Joseph Mercola, a health advocate on nutrition, recommends a daily fibre intake of 25 to 50 grams per 1,000 calories consumed.

9. Get a proper balance of grains, protein, and fats. This means be sure to add in healthy fats. Healthy fats in moderation do not make you fat. Healthy fats include: raw nuts, coconut oil, avocados, olive oil, fish oil, raw seeds, organic eggs, organic meat, raw cheese.

10. When possible, eat organic and grass fed. Of course, it's a personal choice, and budget can be a concern, but it is clear that organic foods are less chemically polluted and, with animal sourced food, better environments are provided for livestock. The documentary *Food Inc.* illustrates important information for consumers. The book, *Food Politics* by Marion Nestle, is a great reference as well.

11. Make it a habit to read nutrient and ingredient labels. Most importantly, check for the grams of sugar in items. According to Dr. Robert Lustig, a neuroendocrinologist who has done extensive research on the role of sugar in your body, your liver can only safely metabolize about six teaspoons of added sugar per day. Any excess gets metabolized into body fat. Dr. Joseph Mercola recommends limiting daily fructose intake to 25 grams (approximately six teaspoons) or less from all sources, including natural sources such as fruit. Note: 25 g is equal to approximately 2.5 medium sized apples.

Please consider that 'fake' sugar and artificial sweeteners are not a worthy replacement. According to Elson M. Haas, MD, author of *Staying Healthy with Nutrition*, "this substance can be a neurological irritant and can affect users' mood and energy." Natural alternative sweeteners include fruit and stevia.

12. Keep a food log. It is beneficial for accountability and awareness.

Losing weight (or gaining if we are underweight) does not bring us happiness, nor is it long lasting if we focus on nutrition alone.

Habit #2: Nutrition

We are intelligent creatures and require much more knowledge in order to put our engine together and get it running. We have to remove some of the artificial happiness stimulants that blur our vision.

The same can be said for exercise, or 'movement'. That one component is simply that (a component). It may be interesting, it may bring you enjoyment, but as a part of the complete happiness package, it cannot exist by itself.

Taking the time to understand each step of the process, and putting them altogether to customize your life, will bring you happiness. That process of building will instill a sense of appreciation that will never leave you.

Before you move on to the other habits, set a new positive commitment for nutrition. When you commit to change, remove one unwanted 'habit' and replace it with a wanted habit. Then, the following week, ask yourself what you can do to stretch yourself. When you identify what you can do, expand on that new practice by selecting something else in the category of nutrition. What's one new nutritious food that can be introduced? What unhealthy food can you choose to remove? What are some new healthy recipes you can test?

Fill in the blanks: In my commitment to following the steps, and taking baby steps toward inner-happiness, I know I will arrive at my healthy-size. One aspect of this will be to eat something I totally enjoy and not feel guilty. In doing this I will not feel deprived, and will appreciate balance by enjoying a small amount of _____ and truly savouring each bite. And I will incorporate _____ and _____ into my day, in order to advance myself toward total wellness and inner-happiness.

Eat Jane, Eat

So I began with movement, which I mostly hoped would work as my start to creating true inner-happiness. I based that hope mostly on my confidence in Grace, not in myself. It went better than I thought. That's because I chose something I enjoyed. When I was a kid I loved the freedom of walking and running. As a child, on a farm, I loved building up speed and feeling the wind in my hair as I ran past the paddock and toward the creek.

I took the price tags off the training shoes and laced up; partly wishing they wouldn't fit and I'd have to postpone. What a ninny. But they fit perfectly. And so I walked around the block. It wasn't a full on run with the wind in my hair, but it wasn't a mad race around Costco either. It was unhindered; there was enough breeze to remind me of happier days of freedom.

The kids had sat on the front step and watched me. One block.

A couple of hours later, when my older one assured me they'd be okay for fifteen minutes, I went around the block again, and then the next block, circling past home in a figure eight to make sure the house hadn't burned down. Then I went again. A slow jog it was not, but it was faster than the first time around. And I walked every day for the next ten days—found ways to make the time for it.

One night, about a week later, when the kids were in bed, I opened the fridge and really looked at what I was feeding us. I read labels; couldn't even pronounce some of the ingredients.

I thought about my commitment to my future, so I took the salad dressing, because it had the longest list, and poured it down the drain. I rinsed the bottle for the recycling, but then whipped outside and grabbed a long-stemmed daisy. I put it in the bottle. "This is for me," I said.

My resolve to limit sugar and be mindful of how much junk I ate made the next five days brutal. I had a constant headache. Tap water tasted horrible. I wanted soda pop. Driving by the regular fast food drive-thru was painful, but I did not stop there. Those were changes I'd committed to. Easy on the sugar. Water instead of soda. No daily stop at Timmies for coffee and donuts. I knew, if I went through the drive-thru for coffee, I'd order a donut as well. A few changes and I already felt like I could fail instantly.

I second guessed my commitment to Grace. I was nothing but a loser. I hunted up some Tylenol. I stared at a box of cookies. I had waves of feeling, even almost knowing, that I was going to give up. But I didn't. I'd told her I would 'commit' and am going to trust this process. I licked the illustration of the cookie. It made me think, if I'd been seen licking cardboard, I'd be taken in for psychiatric examination.

I was the seven dwarfs from hell all in one horrible mother: irritable, impatient, grumpy, annoyed, short, testy. On day four, I got someone to take my volunteer shift at the kids' school because I was worried I'd blow up at anyone who said anything more than good morning—and totally lose it if I heard a recorder. "Is this what it's like to withdraw from cocaine?" I asked myself.

My daughter—I can tell the difference between my children's printing—made a sign that said ENTUR AT YOUR OWEN RISK. She actually taped it outside on the front door. I tore it off. I went on the internet and read a study that said sugar is eight times more addictive than cocaine. I was a junkie.

I kept the portion sizes the same at mealtimes, not wanting to change too much at once. But I still wanted something sweet. Two weeks in, I went to the store and picked up frozen berries and a bag of chia seeds. Chia seeds for chrisssakes. Who is this person that now buys chia seeds? Came home, made chia jam. A cup of bagged frozen fruit, defrosted, mixed with two tablespoons of chia seeds in a mug. Left it in the fridge overnight. The next morning, I made a chia jam sandwich. Oh joy! I had something that resembled the jelly in a donut, but it was sharper, had more raspberryish flavour.

I found some herbal tea bags at the back of the one cupboard I'd decided to clean out. Wow, flavourful. And having a hot beverage didn't make me miss my friend coffee quite so much… or rather, my fix. Caffeine.

The headache eased. My son won a water bottle at school and gave it to me. I took it as his knowing I was making an effort. I cried, excessively. Scared the heck out of him. "Tears of joy," I assured him. "Tears of joy."

I mounted it on a fanny-pack thing Jack had brought home from a golf tournament. And I wore it on walks. Actual walks for which I arranged a sitter or trade-offs with friends. When the sitter arrived two Saturday afternoons after my first chia jam sandwich, I filled my water bottle, popped an apple and a chia jam sandwich in the fanny pack, laced up my runners, walked to a nearby nature trail, entered the pathway, and jogged. Yes, jogged.

Go Jane, Go. I pictured the title above the whimsical illustration on the iconic primer.

The next three weeks were interesting: progress, two tragedies, and some drama. But I learned some things about myself. There were triggers. When my mother phoned and asked for the tenth time why we couldn't make the drive back to visit, I took ten minutes of her nosiness, then feigned a static line and hung up. I trekked down to the basement freezer and unearthed a half-slab of stale birthday cake. Ate the entire flavourless brick. All of it. Even chewed and swallowed a piece of wax from the candle before realizing what it was. Couldn't even remember whose birthday it was from.

Another time, when the kids were fighting, and getting ready for school, I opened the tax bill, burst into tears, and searched the house, unsuccessfully, for caffeinated soda.

When I couldn't find one, I decided I'd go to Timmies—I deserved a coffee and donut. But, when I tripped over my running shoes, I laced up, drove the kids to school, parked at the nature trail, jogged through the pathway still cool with morning dew, and took an exit I'd not seen before. It came out at a little independent café that used to be a horse stable. I sat outside at a table, ordered an herbal tea on ice. With the kids still at school, I detoured through another part of the park, saw a white-tailed deer and a fox. The pine trees smelled great. A couple of people waved to me. A biker rang his bell when he passed me. I called out a thank you. He called out a "you're welcome". The exchange felt like an entirely satisfying conversation.

I stopped at the store on the way home for gluten free bread. It was something I could have instead of the white sandwich slices I'd been putting the delicious chia jam on.

I hated myself a few times. I hated that there seemed to be no instant (and lasting) results of easy-life feeling, of happiness, of joy, of calm, and of weight loss. And I hated myself for previously being sucked into the marketing game of weight loss and fitness. I cast a spell on all the unethical sugar pushers all over the world.

Those moods passed. I thought about ways to deal with my mom's commentary on my aunt's divorce, her neighbour's gout or goat —I never listened that well—and, of course, I dwelled on my crumbling marriage. I came up with a less hectic plan to make the kids' transition to after-school activities easier on all of us.

My water bottle became my buddy. My sneakers: partners who were twins. I found a fantastic morning route that was populated by serious runners—who called out greetings and made me feel welcome. I felt like a bit of an outsider taking up space on their path, and wondered if they thought that of me too.

I felt ten years younger when I walked, jogged, ran. More importantly, I felt free. There was no finish line. There was no measurement of kilometres traveled. Only peace and freedom. And oxygen. Oh, how my brain had missed breathing.

Then my youngest wanted a water bottle like mommy's. I picked up one for each of the kids, but when I began to squeeze apple juice from the tetra pack, wonder of wonder, they both pointed to the tap.

I kept things fairly regular for the kids, but had replaced a few foods with long ingredient lists with fresh fruit. I kept their juice boxes: apple, orange, pineapple. It was fruit, I reasoned until I later noticed how much sugar was actually in just one juice box. From that moment on it was natural soda with lime. I also managed to find granola bars with six grams of sugar or less, and baked chips with no artificial stuff. I researched. I read. I discerned. I was truly becoming informed. I wanted my kids to eat healthier, and in 'calling out' the ingredients I was learning to voice a truth.

I returned to the nature park with the kids. We took a picnic. They loved it, as did I.

But, with all these successes and newness-es, I still felt odd. I realized that I'd need to find other ways to deal with unmet career needs, schedules, and being at the stale end of a marriage. I missed my career. I craved the satisfaction that came from analysis, and was intrigued by the role of advocacy. I longed for the way Jack and I used to be. Junk food was not an option because I was proud of my commitment. Movement helped. I noticed my clothes were looser. I had more energy. But, I still didn't know how to completely relax.

Through my struggles I identified a few things to be aware of. I made a list.
1. Usually, I can't eat just one of something, so I'm better off not having any than just one because otherwise it turns into a whole bag.

2. I am good throughout the day, but the evening is when I need to find distractions other than food.
3. I regress on 'girls-nights-out' and that causes relapses for me. But I need some adult conversation, not just the whining and demands of children.

I planned to speak to the four friends I had a once a month girls-night-out with, to see if we could include an activity, or at least go to The Stable Café where they had gluten free chocolate cake. I didn't know how they'd take that. I held off. I didn't want them to break up with me.

I never missed a session with Grace. And I knew what was coming up. I didn't know how I'd fit the next Step into my day. At least meditation wasn't asking me to stop eating something or to climb a mountain; it would be asking me to 'be a mountain' or sit on a mountain or something like that. Spirituality. Oh, God!

Habit #3: Spiritual Practice

Wikipedia defines modern spirituality as being centered on the "deepest values and meanings by which people live." It embraces the idea of an ultimate or an alleged immaterial reality. It envisions an inner path enabling a person to discover the essence of his/her being.

The essence of you.

Does that word 'essence' and that phrase create a warm feeling inside?

In our essence we are spiritual beings having a human experience.

In practicing various ways to get to know yourself and your values, and then expressing yourself and honouring your values, know that:

Each person is unique; therefore, what practice works for one person may not work for another. Be open to all, and then apply what resonates for you.

When you've evaluated what will work for you, it is best to focus on one spiritual practice than to focus on many. Put simply, go deep instead of wide.

Spiritual practice is intended to be a meaningful experience, not just something done by 'going through the motions'—feel it from inside.

Spiritual practice progresses with maturity, in stages, levels, and steps.

Habit #3: Spiritual Practice

GRATITUDE

Be thankful for what you have; you'll experience more.

Feeling and showing appreciation is something we can do in every moment, because, once practiced, it becomes a way of being. When we appreciate what we have, it opens the door to receiving more. It's equally important to hold gratitude for what is within us, as well as what is around us.

Focusing on the false illusion of greener grasses, along with preconceived ideals of a fulfilled life, keeps us from experiencing total contentment. To experience true contentment, focus not on what is missing in our lives, but rather on our gratitude for what we do have, and for unexpected opportunities. When we spend time concentrating only on unrealized success, we miss out on so many blessings and 'mini' successes that have already occurred. It feels like life just passes us by when we constantly 'prepare' for the one big success, pushing out further the end goal.

Being grateful for at least three things each day that involves self, career, personal life, and relationships is life changing; like opening the door to our souls which allows positive energy to flow both outward and inward in our lives.

Gratitude keeps us focused on joy and abundance in our current life.

One way to work on the gratitude habit—which is a spiritual practice—which takes each of us inside and helps us identify with our core values, is to start a gratitude journal. Jotting down five things you are grateful for (each day), pen to paper. When we recognize and appreciate things we take for granted, life begins to fall into place, meaning is expanded, and life grows exponentially with fulfillment and happiness.

Being grateful raises the level of Dehydroepiandrosterone (DHEA), a hormone which offsets the stress hormone, cortisol

(cortisol is produced during stress or fight or flight). Being grateful not only satisfies, on a mental level, it helps the body feel good on a physical level.

PRAYER

Prayer is another word for a statement linked to faith, or an affirmation. "Say a prayer for me", is a common request, and simply means, "think of me".

'Sending prayers', relates to thinking kind thoughts. Many people use prayer as a key component of their faith. At its core, it is a link with the wonder and energy of life.

Making statements to ask for something for someone, or for one's self, or to thank a power that is greater than us, is a part of spiritual practice that is incredibly individual. And it is very powerful.

There is an array of rituals that involve prayer. Some may describe the power of prayer and the outcomes as miraculous, others may say it is karma, and yet others find it an unexplainable but necessary practice. Put simply, prayer is an expression of faith—chants, poetry, song, and a heart-felt inner voice—that involves asking and receiving with complete conviction.

Faith in nature, science, wonder, or all three? Perhaps they are the same thing. Prayer doesn't have to be something we learned in Sunday School—but it certainly can be. Prayer can be a statement of faith in oneself and the larger picture. A greater power.

Remember, the prayer we ask for may not come in the form we expect or when we expect it, because it is always answered in a way to help serve our authentic self and our purpose, not our ego. We will not receive more until we first learn to appreciate what we have on our plate. We may not like what is on our plate (and be looking for dessert), but take time to look, first, for the lesson.

Habit #3: Spiritual Practice

MEDITATION AND/OR YOGA

Oh, for a tranquil place for the heart to rest. A soft place on which to fall. The silence in the chaos. The ability to reach a higher, peaceful level within the self. A place to be still. A time to silence the voice of ego and to listen to authentic 'self'.

Meditation allows us to clear energy blocks and align to the energy force of the universe. It brings our physical and mental body in tune with our spiritual body. It helps us to become more mindful and aware of the current moment which improves our day to day well-being by bringing the body in to harmony.

Mediation and yoga allows each person to fuel his or her mind, spirit and body without food. To draw upon positive energy that already exists costs us nothing, and simply waits within to be accessed—like the water from a clear spring.

Often misunderstood, meditation conjures up visions of gurus, sitting on mountain tops in India. Not many of us have been taught that meditation, or the practice to be still, is a necessary function of a full life and, therefore, like other practices, we avoid it. Even frown upon it. Sometimes mock it.

Some people avoid it because it seems like work. Something else to learn. The amazing thing is there isn't anything to learn. There is simply an unwinding as we unlearn and fall into a complete state of relaxation in order to connect and listen to our inner spirit.

The art of meditation allows every one of us to connect to the divine source of spirit. Spirit is often confused with the word religion. If that's something you think, commit to opening your mind and heart, and go deep inside and experience a simple meditation.

Theologians will explain that, regardless of the main religions—Buddhism, Christianity, Judaism, Islam, and Hindi—each has similar fundamentals. Just different names for their gods, and different rituals.

The common denominator is faith, not religion.

The beauty of meditation is that it is free. It is available at any minute of the day. We can perform short or long meditations. We are in control of this spiritual alignment we experience through meditation, and we do not have to wait on anyone else for it.

When we don't meditate or create a spiritual practice, we may find that we feel an emptiness, and then, because we've not been trained to recognize that emptiness as a need to reconnect with our inner-self, we feel we have to find something to fill it. This misinterpretation often results in a need to eat or drink or shop or gamble or hurt ourselves—yes, artificial stimulation.

Aiming for daily meditation or 'being still' is a fantastic goal. Ten minutes is enough, though it is blissful to have a bit longer, even thirty minutes. Our excuse? We don't have the time. Yet, most of us can blow much more than that on social media. So, we do have the time. We have ten minutes.

Because we are encouraging baby steps to move through creating many new habits, and you have a lot to think about, you might want to choose to meditate for ten minutes every other day.

How? Well, there are all kinds of meditations that are led by various meditators. You can find them through 'social media'. But the easiest one is to put down the device and simply breathe.

Super simple, for 10 minutes.

1. Get comfortable in a quiet place where you will not be interrupted, and close your eyes.
2. Breathe in and out and notice your breaths (if your mind wanders just bring it back to the breathing; take a few deep breaths and exhales).

Habit #3: Spiritual Practice

3. Allow your breathing to be comfortable/normal/relaxed.
4. Notice each part of your body relax, thank each part of body for its function, and picture light entering it.
5. Pay attention to your thoughts. Do not drive them. Instead, pay attention to information that comes through you. Trust your inner knower. Your intuition. Just listen.
6. Bring your breathing back to several deep inhales and exhales and open your eyes.

If that feels like too much to start, begin with just breathing.

Meditation is to be, not to do. Because we are simply 'being' in a meditation, we discover our link to nature. And therefore, time spent in natural environments is also spiritual. Sitting in a garden and focusing on the scent of a flower in bloom can be a meditation.

Spending time in nature has been proven to fill our spiritual being and to ground us.

The time doesn't have to be long. 'Micro-breaks' with nature, even just looking at pictures, has discernible benefits for our minds.

WHAT ARE CHAKRAS?

In our Western world, we experience a great deal of physical wealth. In contrast, there is a prevalence of spiritual poverty. Violence and negativity dominates our news. Fear and unhappiness torment the majority of the population. Mind-numbing materialism consumes the resources. There is a great void left to be filled.

One way to fill that void and create spiritual balance is by understanding our energy chakras. Chakra balancing meditation can be very beneficial to help create a sensation of balance and help achieve mental clarity and spiritual fullness.

Collateral Happiness: The Power Behind the Facade

Chakras are like junctions between mind, body and spirit which link our physical, energetic, emotional, mental, social, and spiritual selves. Balancing chakras helps bring our complete being toward balance, health, and well-being. Likewise, if our being experiences imbalance, it causes blocks in the chakras. They are traditionally thought of as spinning vortices of energy and are located at different levels in the body, along the base of the spine, and ending at the top of the head. There are seven main chakras in the body, each one specific in function. Clearing our energy chakras can be very beneficial to increasing energy flow in the body, which allows for increased body, mind, and spirit balance. This can be done through Reiki or Chakra balancing meditations.

Chakra	Function	Vibration	Colour	Location	Counterforce
Root	Survival	"Lam"	Red	Base of Spine	Fear
Sacral	Pleasure/ Creativity	"Vam"	Orange	Pelvis area	Guilt
Solar Plexus	Power/ Identity	"Ram"	Yellow	Stomach area	Shame
Heart	Love	"Yam"	Green	Heart area	Grief
Throat	Communication	"Ham"	Blue	Throat area	Dishonesty
Third Eye	Intuition	"Om"	Indigo	Brow area	Illusion
Crown	Consciousness	"Ah"	Purple/ White	Top of Head	Attachment

The seven chakras are related to our basic human birthrights. Right to exist, right to feel, right to act freely, right to love and be loved, right to speak and hear truth, right to see and trust intuition, and right to know. When any of these rights are threatened by fear of violation or loss, we feel out of balance with our being and feel disconnect throughout our body and corresponding chakras.

Habit #3: Spiritual Practice

In reviewing prayer, gratitude, and meditation, what might you commit to this week and continue as a practice?

1. What commitment can you make about gratitude (journal, meditation)?
2. What might your daily prayer or affirmation be?
3. What is your daily or every other day meditation practice going to be?

It's possible to combine these. Get creative. You deserve the experience of the inner you.

PRACTICAL PRACTICE

Schedule time to take five minutes, today, to breathe. Let the thoughts come and go.

Look into local meditation groups. Attending a session may help you get used to the feel of meditation and get yourself out there.

Habit #4: Creativity/Learning

The ability for each of us to expand our mind is critical to our success. By dedicating ourselves to learning, and embracing creativity—yes, we have it—we can get ahead in every aspect of life. All it takes is a commitment.

THE IMPORTANCE OF CREATIVITY

Creativity thrives in an environment of confidence and inner-security. This is why it is important to build inner-confidence, be self-assured, and self-centered, because expressing creative energy entails doing things that are unconventional. At times we may be the lone nut standing outside the crowd and it takes a certain level of confidence to be willing to do so.

Creative energy demands expression and release. It leaps tall buildings, moves past mountains, and obliterates obstacles. It cannot be contained. This force of energy has the ability to be directed in positive or negative ways.

Positive creativity can be expressed as a dancer who performs before a crowd or an entrepreneur who creates a solution to a problem. Negative creativity can be directed in terms of con artists who connive to cheat us out of our hard earned money.

When being different, out of place, or mediocre causes us to feel inferior, we repress our creative energy and tend to veil or hide our insecurity. Essentially we erect a facade—become inauthentic. We worry that we might appear foolish, and thus stifle creative release which, of course, exacerbates inner turmoil.

Habit #4: Creativity/Learning

Insecurity, fear of rejection, and need for approval represses creative energy. The result of repression eventually manifests in an eruption—it has to expel a build-up of obstruction somehow—as overeating, drinking, excessive spending, gambling, drug use. Blocked creative energy emerges as forms of depression, anxiety, inner turbulence, or other body or mind problems.

Creativity generates within us an innate desire to be unique, yet it's repressed by our strong desire for love and connection—to fit in. This poses an inner-conflict and dilemma.

The intention is not to be one hundred percent confident in our uniqueness but to be willing and able to tolerate vulnerability. The intention is also to build inner-confidence through practice, learning, and skill development not through external validation and approval.

Typically, once we acknowledge, confront and move past a sense of insecurity—despite fears—we find clarity and inner harmony with a positive release of creativity. That's when we move past mountains.

It is important to understand here that skillful execution of creativity takes practice (therefore, time) and learning. Many times people nip creativity in the bud because they don't get it right at first and the insecurity comes through. Then they think they are not creative or worthy of expressing it.

The key is to develop the necessary degree of skill to create a level of confidence in which talent and creativity flows. **Learning is paramount in developing skill that is required for this full creative expression. It also helps us to expand beyond our current limiting beliefs resulting in a higher sense of self.**

It is so important to find the confidence to stand out in a crowd. Taking the time to learn a craft, in depth not breadth, results in fulfillment. When we learn to master a skill, we develop the confidence which allows us to release our truest form of creative energy flow.

Before we can inspire others with our creativity, we have to find the confidence to allow our 'energy' to flow into the world. This is why movement becomes so important because, while we develop the confidence to express creative 'energy', we can release any extra 'energy' through movement.

People have the potential of tapping into undiscovered creative ideas and projects within. Floodgates of creative energy open when people overcome the need for the approval of others.

The key is to overcome insecurity by understanding how to overcome fears and stand outside your comfort zone.

- Find positive ways to channel your creative energy.
- Establish daily movement.
- Spend time in nature.
- Incorporate learning (skill/craft) into each day.

EXPAND YOUR MIND

Those dedicated to continuous learning take in their information in various ways including reading, taking courses, attending conventions, participating in brainstorming sessions, and listening to podcasts. Through this they stay current, and their knowledge of past and present as well as future trends increases.

Three kinds of learning focused upon here are: maintenance learning, growth learning, and shock learning.[1]

1) Maintenance Learning

Maintenance learning represents keeping pace in order to prevent falling behind. It is reading an occasional book and keeping current with blogs and newsletters. Essentially the information we acquire only 'maintains' our knowledge but does not expand our experience or skill.

Habit #4: Creativity/Learning

We can 'get by' with maintenance learning for a while. There will come a point in time when we will find ourselves bored and seeking more. We might feel listless and not know why. It is the body's way of telling us it's time to grow.

We often find ourselves in this situation with jobs we've been at for 5, 10, 20+ years, or when we perform manual jobs which require mundane, repetitive action. Many people lose their sense of happiness in these situations because they talk themselves into staying for the money. If people decide to stay in such a role, it is necessary to find another skill or craft to learn, in depth, in their personal life.

When we tire due to maintenance learning, and there is no potential for advancement, we need to make a decision as to how growth can be incorporated into learning.

2) Growth Learning

This is the kind of learning that adds knowledge and skills to our repertoire that we did not have before.

Growth learning helps us expand the mind. It entails acquiring information that we did not previously have.

There are great sources of inspiration for growth learning. The key is to find a craft or a skill we wish to develop. We can discover great ideas by listening to podcasts, reading blogs, and reading books. We can learn incredible information without having to buy anything at all. Many universities and colleges offer their curriculum for free in many subject areas. That means the material is available at no cost, to download—no professor, but the learning opportunity remains.

Shadowing someone at their work is also an amazing and no-cost learning experience. Wine and food enthusiasts can find classes and tastings in which to grow culinary knowledge.

Growth learning can be personal-interest related and does not only have to be to advance 'career'.

Dedicate Yourself To Continuous Education

Our ability to expand the mind and devote ourselves to lifelong learning is the key to breaking any success barriers. If (or when) we find ourselves at a place in life where there is no door open, we may want to consider taking the time to grow our skill or hone our craft further.

Aim to read 30 minutes/day, 6-7 days a week. Fiction, non-fiction, biographies, personal growth books are all meaningful. Ted talks and Inspirational videos are an excellent way to sneak in more information. Watching 'Prove Them Wrong' from Be Inspired Channel, or 'Happiness' on TED, helps to retrain the mind to remain positive and motivated.

It's also important for each of us to spend time learning about ourselves. The road to ultimate happiness is learning what makes us happy both inside and outside.

What can you commit to this week to incorporate learning or creativity into your life? What skill or gift do you want to develop in depth?

Is there anything (people, time, reservations, limiting beliefs, negative habits) holding you back? What are you afraid of giving up?

3) Shock Learning

Shock learning contradicts or reverses knowledge or understanding that we already have.

Peter Drucker, in *Innovation and Entrepreneurship*, explains that we learn to be innovative when we are shocked by unexpected occurrences.

Habit #4: Creativity/Learning

Shock can provide an opportunity for new growth if we learn to welcome the unexpected instead of cursing it. Most people do not like change. When something happens that is completely unexpected, many choose to ignore it or resist it to appease the biological response of survival to stay comfortable.

Controlling or preventing change is an illusion. Life will always change around us. We can embrace it as opportunity, or dismiss it as threat.

Constant change is educational; opportunity for growth.

If you do not have a hobby, now is a great opportunity to consider options and find one that you enjoy. Embrace it, hone your skills, learn, practice and allow yourself to become great at it. Commit to it. Having a hobby is not just about occupying your time. It also allows you to 'learn', and it releases creative energy flow, both of which are critical in creating collateral happiness.

---

[1] (source: https://www.briantracy.com/blog/personal-success/expand-your-mind-importance-of-lifelong-learning-and-continuous-education/)

Habit #5: Positive Relationships

Harvard conducted a 75 year study on emotional well-being and identified that those who maintained happiness and health in their lives held positive relationships.

It is important to become conscious of the energy levels of our acquaintances, friends, and family. Choose to be in relationships with people who are empowering, inspiring, who see greatness in us, and who bring out a higher vibrational energy in us. When it comes to relationships, we are greatly influenced—positively or negatively—by those closest to us. People in our lives will directly influence how we think, feel and act—good or bad. If we spend the majority of our time with unhappy people, we will likely be influenced to be unhappy.

Current studies prove that emotions affect the world around us. HeartMath researchers have shown that the physical aspects of DNA strands can be influenced by human intention.

https://www.heartmath.org/articles-of-the-heart/personal-development/you-can-change-your-dna/

In the presence of positive emotions, coils of DNA relax. In the presence of negative emotions, DNA tightens. Researchers have concluded that "human emotion produces effects which defy conventional laws of physics."

As humans we have something called mirror neurons which can cause a release of dopamine. The mirror neurons allow us to pick up emotional energy, like an infectious laugh or smile. If we smile at others it triggers their mirror neurons to make them smile back. Smiling helps to release dopamine which in turn means we can affect someone else to feel good.

Habit #5: Positive Relationships

To test this theory, smile at someone for 10 seconds and lock gaze. Do they smile back? It is difficult and takes work to hold back a smile if someone is smiling at us. Likewise, a scowl or frown can cause a reciprocal negative expression.

Surrounding ourselves with positive influences, and positively influencing others, is a key to happiness. Our emotions can physically change the world around us simply through mirror neurons and DNA.

Motivational speaker Jim Rohn famously said that we are the average of the five people we spend the most time with.

Take a moment to think about this. This time can include people in the same room as us, people we spend time watching on TV and/or videos, and even people we spend time reading books about. If we want to be happy, it is important to choose to spend the majority of your time with happy people.

Each one of us carries ingrained, unconscious ideas of just how happy and successful we can be. Author of *The Big Leap*, Gay Hendricks, states that by learning to identify and transcend self-imposed 'Upper Limits', we can expand our potential for happiness and abundance in amazing ways. Sometimes we are afraid to open ourselves to new, empowering relationships, not because of the uncertainty of the new, but because doing so causes us to feel disloyalty and abandonment towards current relationships.

This barrier is the feeling that 'I cannot expand to my full success' because it would cause me to end up all alone, be disloyal to my roots and leave behind people from my past. **Another reason it may be difficult to change relationships is because we are afraid to outshine others.** We tell ourselves, we can't shine too much, or we'll make others feel bad or look bad, and thus we stay in our comfortable relationships. In both of these situations, it is important to recognize that people who are truly positive influences will support us no matter what.

To move forward, we don't just need courage to embrace the 'future unknown', but need to find the courage to leave behind the familiarity of the old.

When we are engaged in these limiting beliefs, or 'Upper-Limits', we stall the flow of happy and positive energy. It is important to be aware of these beliefs so we can recognize and stop ourselves from limiting our current and future relationships.

Sometimes we need to remember: 'It's better to say something than to say nothing at all.' Growing up, we may have been hurt or taught to hold our tongue and not speak up.

~~~~~

Most people create rules around feeling loved, or connected, or included, by making it dependent upon the behaviors and actions of **other people.**

It may seem odd, but most women, without realizing, often expect their partners to be mind-readers; anticipating these partners to guess and initiate whatever the women are thinking (the outcome of which will provide the women a feeling of being loved). Most partners are not mind-readers. This kind of expectation sets off a cycle of 'he doesn't love me' syndrome.

In the case of mind-reading it is exampled by 'I feel loved when someone reads my mind and knows to rub my feet and put the kids to bed'.

We also create rules where we only feel loved if someone else comes and **loves us first**.

For example, I only feel loved if someone: 'phones me and says they need me', 'brings homemade jelly to me (first before I reciprocate)'.

It is important to expand our rules to have many, not just one. It is also important to be in control of your own love.

Habit #5: Positive Relationships

Here's the best idea on this topic:

create rules that are not dependent on others.

These rules begin with 'I feel loved when I _____'(insert action).

For example, I feel loved when:
- **I give someone a hug or a kiss.**
- **I invite a friend over for dinner.**
- **I tell someone that I love them.**
- **I hold someone's hand.**
- **I create an emotional and engaging conversation with someone.**

These are 'my' actions versus waiting for someone else's actions.

When we are confident, fulfilled, and in charge of our own 'department of love', we can create loving relationships on our own terms.

A favourite question I ask clients is, "What do you specifically need in order to feel loved by your partner, your friend, your mother...?" Most clients do not actually have an answer on the tip of their tongue.

We often easily identify what we don't want, but spend little time thinking about what we actually do need. Once we identify what we need, we can relay that need to people we have relationships with, and when someone knows what you need instead of making them guess, and if you are in control of your own love, your love increases exponentially.

We limit our capacity to feel love if we do not put ourselves in control of the actions. In order to feel love and connection from other people we are required to define love for ourselves, establish that we can ask for what we need, and that we can give love to others in various ways: a hug, inviting someone for a visit, sending a positive note.

Collateral Happiness: The Power Behind the Facade

When we are clear that we are in control of our need to connect with others, we are freer and experience much more satisfaction.

Push through the fears and discomfort. Do it for necessary growth. Question personal beliefs. How do they serve us? Speak true thoughts and feelings in order to release them, in order to move on.

When it comes to relationships, be aware that sometimes we are not always the ones getting hurt.

Sometimes, without intention, we are the ones who are hurting others.

These are the times that we need to set our egos aside and allow the other person to open up and his or her feelings. We need to improve communication in order to understand what we can do to make a relationship better, so we can increase connection. The best way to do that is to stick to facts, do not insult, and share true feelings.

Most of the time, conflict in relationships is due to someone reading between the lines, filling in the blanks, and misunderstanding the other person. Don't be afraid to ask for clarification. Do not assume.

Seize the opportunity of experiencing a happy relationship by listening to advice. When people have the courage to provide feedback, be respectful of it. Listen. Don't speak over them. There's no need to feel offended. Mentors and guides in our lives are valuable resources. The only difference between feedback and criticism is how we perceive it.

Make loved ones a priority. Honour the 'self'. Relationship maintenance is essential to creating collateral happiness.

Habit #5: Positive Relationships

What can you do to help yourself regarding learning and relationships?

1. Make a list of all the important people in your life. Ask yourself if you've done anything lately to make them feel loved and important to you. If there is someone you feel you may be neglecting, write down one or two things you can do in the next week to show them your love and appreciation.

2. What are your current rules with regard to feeling love? Do you know what you need in order to feel loved? Do you know what your partner needs? How can you be in control? Start the phrase off with, I feel loved when I...

3. Be sure to schedule weekly time for positive relationships in your life. Do not neglect those closest to you.

Overwhelmed? Already wondering how you will move, eat, learn, love, pray?

Okay, let's review:

Why did you pick up this book?

What do you want from it?

Change takes time and commitment.

Habit #6: Mindfulness

Rest. Relax. Reflect. Release. Reframe. Retrain. Review.

The glorification of busy will destroy us.

Jeff Brown, Author

Taking small steps, not giant leaps, lead to happiness. Many think that to implement R&R means something is sacrificed—as if there will be less time for more important things. This is not true.

Many people make time for TV even in their busy-ness. They have associated downtime with TV. There is time for proper R&R which can come out of the numbing time we waste.

One hour of television—that's one episode of whatever is trending right now—equals some R&R (on a swing in the park?), a fifteen minute meditation, and a chunk of reading.

We are raised with the belief that it is selfish to take time for R&R. According to Dr. Wayne Dyer, women state that their number one priority is family—not making time for themselves first. It's another paradigm shift; people won't change this belief unless out of inspiration or desperation. Those who have experienced burnout know the importance. Those who are still racing the clock to beat the system are neither inspired nor desperate enough to change it.

REST

Sleep is a vital component of success. Necessary for life. The essential partner of awake. There has to be a time when the mind is put

Habit #6: Mindfulness

into another state and begins to do a different kind of work: absorb, let go, file, heal, generate, regenerate, dream.

How much sleep do we need? For some it's 5 hours. For others it's 8 hours. For others it can be 10 hours. We can gauge it by determining if we feel wide awake during the day and can perform all daily activities without problems. If this is the case, then most likely there's enough sleep being had.

It is helpful to determine if we are introverts or extroverts. Introverts do best by recharging their batteries by spending time alone. Extroverts recharge by spending time with others. This is a link for a free personality type test that is based on Carl Jung's and Isabel Briggs Myers' personality type theory.
http://www.humanmetrics.com/cgi-win/jtypes2.asp.
It's also a great test to help understand personality makeup which can help each of us stress out less by better understanding who we are as individuals.

Brain repair and the benefits of restorative sleep are covered here:
http://www.howsleepworks.com/why_restoration.html

RELAX

Means enjoying the present moment, and unwinding into downtime. Relaxing can be inserted into a few deep breaths between busy and next errand; even a second between breaths.

Fitting in relaxation time is about shifting priorities. If you find yourself saying I really should be doing this or that, during a time when you take a break, then it is not a break; many a busy mom, harried salesperson, or dawn to dusk farmer simply believes they're always 'on duty' or 'on call'. Some of us believe that relaxing is laziness—FALSE—it's an investment in self and an act of regeneration.

It can be tough to find time to fit in relaxation into our lives, and the consequences are increased stress and illness. Numerous studies show the increase in sickness and disability in workplaces in the last few decades. Relaxation—in many forms—helps to repair poor interpersonal relationships, poor concentration and judgement.

Learning relaxation techniques can improve quality of life.

If you cannot just sit and relax, and need instruction on how to relax, then you are overdue for relaxation time.

Don't know what qualifies as relaxation? Here's a starter list to get you going.

- Exhale most of the air out of your lungs. Pause. Then, inhale slowly as you count to four. Pause for four seconds and then slowly exhale as you count to four. Repeat.
- Yoga
- Meditation
- Read a chapter in an inspirational book
- Listen to relaxing music
- Soak in the bathtub
- Participate in a hobby
- Enjoy a cup of herbal tea and do nothing except sip and unwind

In order to make time for relaxation:

- Organize and plan your day in advance
- Delegate
- Minimize meeting times by sticking to a time limit
- Get rid of your inner-perfectionist

And take note: many habits can overlap. Spirituality can overlap with exercise. Prepping food can be a sacred time. Learning can overlap with exercise in terms of a walk through nature while listening to a podcast—it's great to combine without overtasking oneself. Start a walk in nature with total silence and appreciation, then continue to walk or jog while listening to an educational podcast, then at the end enjoy nutrition in the company of a good friend (social time). It can all intertwine. One massive spiritually rich, healthy, creative learning experience.

REFLECT

Become self-aware and be more present with your body, mind and spirit all as one being.

A critical step to improving life quality is awareness. Rather than getting too busy, ignoring needs, and avoiding things that bother us, we can take the time to ask what is missing from the happiness formula list.

Think, in isolation, in the mornings or evenings, and for at least 15 minutes every day. Consider beginning a journal. Bullet points, doodles, drawings—it doesn't have to be an essay. Journaling helps to get thoughts out on paper and helps you reflect. Write a single word on your paper calendar that is a positive word; that qualifies as minimalistic journaling.

Take a look at the happiness formula each day and ask yourself if you are happy and if you are neglecting anything on the formula. Stay on top of it. Brainstorm with yourself about what needs on your list have to be addressed in your life and what you can do. Ask questions to self.

Once you reflect and become aware, you can make the choice to determine if you need to 1) release negative energy, thoughts or habits, 2) retrain your mind with new positive energy, thoughts or habits or 3) reframe your negative thought with a new positive thought.

RELEASE

Release any negative energy from your life and your body. Let go of that which clutters the spaces in your mind and where you live.

- Do this through visualization.
- Do it by writing a list on paper and burning it.
- Do it by imagining blowing all your frustration into a balloon, tying it off, and releasing it into the air to drift away.
- Hold an imaginary dandelion in seed and blow all the tufts of the plant into the breeze.
- Squeeze your shoulders and release them, feeling the burden ease within your head and shoulders and back.
- Bring the concept of release into part of your meditation so that you get the opportunity to release each time you meditate.

RETRAIN

Retraining is simply being conscious, each day, about breaking old habits and replacing them with the new habits of happiness. Awareness or consciousness can be simply wearing a bracelet (choosing a talisman) to help you remember your commitment. Something that jingles when you move about or tense up. Retraining is not a negative word. Many find it useful to include the word refreshing, as in cleansing the brain/body of old habits, much like we do when we update our computers.

REFRAME

Learning to recognize your ego's voice, and training yourself to pause and reframe your thoughts, is absolutely necessary to reach inner-happiness. It takes time to listen to negative messages and catch yourself inside them, and reframe them. (I am fat. No, I am a human on the road to a completely healthy and happy life.) When you find yourself in a negative thought pattern, reframe it by starting off with things like, "I am on the path to...", or, "I am working toward... "

Habit #6: Mindfulness

When we reframe, we need to first recognize and become aware of our negative 'default' thoughts or habits. Once we become aware, then we need to identify what thought and behavior we want to replace it with. If we do not replace the negative old with positive new, the negative keeps resurfacing. Many times we think about what we don't want, but then forget to replace it with what we do want. It's a good idea to keep a journal of your reframes and to review them. Here are some examples of identifying negative habits and beliefs with a positive reframe.

✘ **Negative Habit:** *Overeat and binge watch TV to recharge and unwind.*

✔ **Reframe:** *I am on my path toward becoming a happier and healthier person. I am working towards releasing overeating and binge watching TV, and am committed towards replacing this pattern with things that include: sitting in my bedroom alone reading my book, using my massager, watching inspirational videos, meditating, taking deep breaths, writing in my journal and drinking a soothing cup of tea.*

✘ **Negative Belief:** *People should love me for me and not for what I look like. I can eat whatever I want. I decide what to eat based on how much I weigh or how fat I look.*

✔ **Reframe:** *If I expect others to love me, then I am going to work towards loving me too. I am on the path toward loving myself and valuing my body. I will decide what to eat based on how I feel, and commit to eating healthy foods and moving my body more.*

✘ **Negative Belief:** *I put my family's needs always before my own. I am selfish and bad if I do not.*

✔ **Reframe:** *I am working toward loving myself and creating happiness which means I am on the path towards putting my needs first. It is self-"care" to look after my own needs as long as it is not at the expense of others.*

✗ **Negative Belief:** *I am always right. I do not like to be questioned or doubted.*

✔ **Reframe:** *Being questioned is not an attack on identity. It is only clarification for more information. Even though I value my own opinions, I will be considerate and aware of the opinions and emotions of other's who differ from me.*

REVIEW

It's important that we each take the time to review lessons and successes, values, goals, purpose and whatever else we want to evaluate. That way we can make adjustments.

Reviewing also helps instill, through repetition, our daily habits, and reminds us how we want to think and act. If we fall out of routine for a day or two, reviewing helps identify where the slip-up happened and what needs to be addressed. Sometimes, when things become habit and they become subconscious, we begin to take them for granted. Reviewing our steps helps us to stay conscious and committed and aware of what we need to focus on.

REVIEW AND TAKEAWAYS

There is no rush to the finish line. We are all on our journey to health and wellness and inner-happiness.

Overwhelming? Don't let it be. Take small steps.

- Move – find ways that you enjoy or re-frame your relationship with exercise.
- Eat. 80/20. Ease up on the sugar. Read labels. Natural food equals natural high.
- Be conscious. Remember the letter R. Rest, relax, release...

PRACTICAL PRACTICE

What result do I want?

What are the consequences of not adding movement?

What negative thought, habit or sacrifice am I willing to give up in order to add movement into my life?

What type of movement can I start to incorporate into my life?

What healthier foods can I start to incorporate into my diet?

What kind of meal plan do I want to follow?

How can I incorporate gratitude into my life?

What is my daily prayer going to be?

What is my daily meditation practice going to be? (sitting and listening to music, guided, making my own, breathing?)

What am I going to commit to for increased growth learning?

Who do I want to spend more time with?

When can I schedule more time for me, family, friends, significant other?

MINDFULNESS AND REFLECTION QUESTIONS

One or two questions a day will build mindfulness and is a simple way to check in on habits.

What were my challenges today?

What were my successes?

Did I take steps today towards my goals? If not, what is preventing me in my internal world?

What were my negative thoughts today? How can I reframe them to be positive?

Is there anything in my life that is out of balance? (habits, self-awareness, self-love, fear) If so, what do I need to address?

Am I experiencing any pain, negative emotions, struggles or challenges? What can I do that is within my control to address this?

Am I following all of my healthy habits? Why or why not?

Do I feel happy today? Why or why not?

What have I learned today?

What is one nice thing I can say to myself today?

What am I prepared to do differently that is not currently serving me in order to improve my life?

What am I willing to release?

What positive influence can I invite into my life?

What new thought, belief or habit do I need to reframe, retrain and focus on?

Am I tired or weak? Do I need to rest?

What story or assumptions have I been telling myself? Is it serving me?

Am I focusing on what I'm missing or what I have?

Am I focusing on what I cannot control or what I can control?

Am I focusing on the past/future or present?

Think Jane, Think

"There's something different about you." My daughter's teacher said it to me in that way when you see someone who always wears glasses, then see them with contacts for the first time.

"Did you cut your hair?" she asked. "You look really great."

My chest closed a bit. It felt so unnatural to hear someone say something nice to me. I wasn't sure I believed her.

"That's when you just reply back with thanks and let someone compliment you," she said. She smiled a row of perfectly even teeth.

My cheeks flushed. "Thanks," I said.

It was still my default thought to feel ugly. And then suddenly Grace's words broke my thought pattern. *I am working toward being a happier and healthier person who is beautiful and loves herself.* Whew, I'd been falling and caught myself. I took a deep breath and smiled back.

The changes I'd made had come together in a bit of an overlap that kept flowing into more changes. And I guess it was working because someone, my child's teacher, noticed. More than that, though. I'd noticed. I had less heartburn, and I was smiling more.

I'd really upgraded my food choices. I still had setbacks; when Jack said he was working late, I'd sometimes catch myself in the pantry reaching for a bag of chips—not as often as before I'd met Grace. Interesting though, that I was still buying them

Collateral Happiness: The Power Behind the Facade

Walking, running, and even hiking had become my 'thing'. I hadn't 'Netflix binged' for a while. I was surprised at myself. The kids and I even walked to the library one day; we all checked-out books. I picked up one on meditation, and I found another one Grace recommended, *The Life You Were Born to Live.*

The meditation one sat for a few days. Closed. Woo-woo scary. When I finally opened it I felt defeated, knew I couldn't sit cross-legged comfortably if my life depended on it. My back hurt just looking at the illustration. Fortunately, I turned the page and found: *what to do if you can't sit cross-legged.* There was a photo of a cushion under the back part of the model's butt. Another diagram simply showed someone sitting upright in a comfortable looking armchair.

So I tried a cushion as a wedge. But, after a few tries, I preferred sitting in the armchair in my bedroom. I'd close the door and sit by myself in my room, in peace and quiet, in the middle of the day. An awkward good at first, but a good nonetheless.

Jack began showing up at home earlier. He'd even eaten supper with us a few nights in a row. His company's financial year-end was over, he announced. Bonuses had been given, and there would be a celebration dinner at a swanky restaurant. I put the last bit out of my mind.

It was a weekend afternoon when I heard him call to the kids to move their bikes. There was general chatter, reminders, threats, and then the lawnmower started up. I pictured the dishes on the kitchen counter, and started to get up. Guilt sat with me a second or too. Then I let it pass. I gave myself permission to put me first. I put in my earbuds, played a relaxing meditation chant, and turned off the outside world.

I'd committed to Grace that I'd meditate for five minutes a day and work up to twenty. Five minutes—one Mississippi-two Mississippi up to three-hundred. Five minutes out of twenty-four hours. How hard could that be?

At first my mind kept wandering—had I put eggs on the grocery list? My mother in law's birthday next week (send card), SUV needs gas, kids both need a dentist appointment. I need an appointment too—but I persevered and kept bringing myself back to my breathing. At one point, the darkness created by closed eyes looked like black velvet with swirling blue light. I trembled, but I kept breathing.

In that first week of meditational attempts, it took five minutes to get past the initial weirdness of it. It was only then I felt myself relax. I took slow, deep, even breaths. I would refocus on my breath each time a thought would start swirling around in my head.

My grade-two-er barged into the room at one point. I ignored him, but felt his stare; opened one eye and could see the puzzled look on his face. He went into my bathroom and rattled around for something in the cupboard. Sunscreen. It overwhelmed my calm. I half breathed to offset the powerful chemicals. The scent wafted away with his exit, and I heard him whisper 'weird'.

It was weird, but I was embracing it and enjoying the relaxation. I quietened my mind.

Then something smashed. It sounded like glass, and the spell was broken. "Moooomm!"

I moved from relaxed to damage-control-mode-mom in three seconds. "No one move," I commanded from the upstairs landing. A pool of white mess flecked with shards of glass pooled on the kitchen floor.

They blamed each other. Their argument in the foreground, lawnmower chopping away in the background; Jack wouldn't have heard the crash or the arguing. I tossed my daughter a pair of shoes so she could step over the mess and get to safety, then began a slow crawl with a rolled bath towel flat on the ground— a bulldozing motion from the edge of the kitchen all the way to the fridge. I truly believe my calmness stopped the kids' argument.

"Pease be more careful next time," I said to both children when my son returned with the shop vac I'd requested.

"You aren't mad, Mom?" he asked.

"No, it was an accident. I've broken many things too. It happens."

The kids looked stunned. I was surprised myself.

And later that night, after I'd turned off the computer, when the kids and Jack were sleeping, I went into the living room and sat on the good sofa. The scent of freshly cut grass filtered through the window screen. I breathed it in. I grabbed Dan Millman's book, *The Life You Were Born To Live*, and opened it to where I had left off yesterday. I wanted to get my thirty minutes of reading in.

When I closed the book, then the window, I wondered what I'd been doing this time a couple of months ago. Having my second Baileys on ice and tuning into late night television while eating a bag of chips? Currently I craved neither fast-food nor film. In fact, nothing I desired was purchasable.

I'd continued to experiment with different times of the day for meditation. Too late and I'd fall asleep. The morning worked well—before anyone was up. It blew me away; I'd usually steal as much time between the sheets as I could until one of the kids stirred.

I'd instituted a locked door policy for my showers. Ten minutes of soapy relaxation and no one peeing or pooping inches from me. No one asking me what was for breakfast. They were not at risk. I deserved the time to myself.

At first they had come to the door and yelled questions, but I'd learned to wait instead of automatically answering.

I thought about those changes as I slid into bed. Jack was snoring. I'd got my thirty minutes of reading in. I placed my hands on Jack's back. His snoring eased.

I was just dozing off. "Mooooom!" It'd been a long day. I was a good person. I'd done my reading, my meditation, walked, eaten well, and still I am asked to suffer.

Up in my daughter's room I asked, "What's the matter?"

"I peed the bed."

"Are you freaking kidding?"

My heart raced. I wanted to scream. In my head all I could think about was how annoyed and frustrated I was. "Go wash up and climb in with Dad," I said

I spoke to the mattress: "Why do the kids automatically yell 'Mom' in these moments? Never 'Dad'?"

I turned on all the lights. Why should I be the only one to suffer? But no one got up. Only I was wide awake, cortisol pulsing through my body. In that instant, I wanted a donut and chips and wine, but there wasn't time—that's what I told myself. Minutes later I'd stripped the bed, put the sheets in the washer, and cleaned up the mess. I huffed and puffed and grumbled as I worked. I wanted a Baileys.

What had happened to the calm Mom who, not long ago, cleaned up broken glass and spilled milk? Was I regressing? Maybe all of this wasn't actually working? Maybe I was doomed to be miserable, impatient, and irritable for the rest of my life.

Somewhere between the laundry room and kitchen pantry my resolve to be strong fell apart.

Crackers, chips, and chocolate. I began munching. Just binge until the rinse cycle, I told myself. But no amount of agitation of the washer could stop the dark thoughts. I took a deep breath. I felt better for one whole second until I realized I had just resorted to my old habit. Instantly, I let the storm of negative thoughts flood in.

Will I ever get this right? Will it ever get easier? What is wrong with me? How could I be Jekyll and Hyde? Calm, cool collected mom by morning and tyrant mom by night. The salty tears mixed with the chip-dust on my lips. I felt so defeated, wanted to crawl in a hole. Wanted to die.

I went to that place. A dark place that looks like a scene out of a *Pirates of the Caribbean* movie. Thoughts were waves tossing the boat from side to side, crashing over the deck and pitching my progress overboard.

Who knows what I was eating when the rinse cycle drained and the washer beeped to signal the end of cycle. I was deaf. The sheets would remain in the washer until the morning. I sank to the floor and sat with the products too large and heavy to go on shelves, and just stayed in the pantry and ate whatever was in my reach, tears rolling down my cheeks until all I could feel was the full heaviness of my stomach. The dark storm had won again.

I wondered how I could see Grace the next day—or officially later that day; it had to be after midnight. How could I tell her that one moment I was calm and the next I had completely regressed?

I could hear the disappointment in her voice already as I pictured myself sitting on her leather chair, a scowl on her face. Maybe I would just call her to make an excuse—a sick child. Yes, okay, I'd decided, that is what I would do. And I'd do it now, at this strange time, so I'd get her voicemail, and it'd be so believable because it was three a.m.

I hung up on the first ring. I had been ready to lie. I hated myself for wanting to lie to the person who was helping me. I had to deal with this. No more running away.

Seven hours later I entered Grace's office with my head hung low.

"What's going on?" she asked.

"You are going to be so disappointed. I completely regressed."

"Disappointed? Are you kidding? I expect you to regress. Do you know how many times I've regressed? Still regress? It's all a part of the process."

It had to be a line. There was no way Grace messed up.

"Jane, I am so proud of you for having the courage to come here today. You have been doing so many great things the past few weeks. Don't let one bad experience override all the good ones. You could never disappoint me."

I wasn't convinced.

"You are human. You are learning. I expect you to have ups and downs. That's how it all works."

Well that was true. I was human. I was learning.

"This process isn't something that happens overnight, or even has a finish line where you graduate and never regress again. The point is not that you never regress. The point is that you came here despite the fact you regressed, and are ready to learn how to get better at picking yourself up and moving on. You have no idea how far you've actually come. I am so proud of you."

I'd never heard her speak so long. She was usually a calm pool of profound questions, punctuated by long pauses that were meant for my answers.

She was happy? Proud? For chrissakes I'd put away at least two bags of chips and at least that in dry ramen noodles. And why was I still buying ramen noodles? I hadn't disappointed her? I was human? That went as far sideways as I had planned.

I eased into the session. I didn't have to go this alone. What a relief I hadn't cancelled the appointment.

I was on my path to creating happiness. I just needed to change the way I thought about it. I needed to change my internal lens so the outside world looked better. The external world doesn't change for me to be happy. My thoughts do—my internal world. I need to focus more on controlling my thoughts and less on controlling everything else around me.

PART IV
GETTING TO KNOW YOU: THE SELF-AWARENESS OF COLLATERAL HAPPINESS

Goals and Commitments
Passion and Purpose
Identifying Core Values
Scheduling and Prioritizing
Self-Limiting Beliefs
Pain and Pleasure
Metaprograms
Changing Our Language
Power of Positive Influence

Step Five: Becoming Self-Aware

To have a conscious knowledge of our own character, understand our feelings and purpose, and know our wishes and desires, is to have self-awareness.

Self-awareness, aka introspection, is the key that opens the door to inner-happiness. The more we understand how we tick, the more we can grow and thrive.

Becoming self-aware is the key to learning who we are. This section is devoted to helping you answer the questions: 'who am I?' and 'who do I want to be?'

Who am I? is often confused with 'what do I do?'

Awareness #1: Goals And Commitments

To reflect balance and harmony in all areas of life, Goals...

- **ultimately help fulfill one of our six needs: love, certainty, variety, significance, growth, contribution.**
- **are substantive and authentic based on how we would like to feel and what we would like to experience.**
- **are best set according to what is within our control, because those goals which are dependent on external forces leave us at the whim of chance, limiting our levels of achievement.**

When we set a goal that fulfills an internal need, we will end up working toward creating internal fulfillment.

Goals which are selfish (things or feelings to be realized or attained at the expense of others, or that which appeases only ego) are not authentically rewarding.

For example: though there is nothing wrong with having a million dollars, the goal of having a million dollars lacks substance. That goal requires back-up: Why a million dollars? What will it allow you to do? To fund? What internal need is it going to fulfill? What experience will it allow you to feel? How are you going to get the million dollars? What will the journey to a million dollars look like and what experiences will it provide?

Material objects, such as money, only serve as a means to the experience or desire. Too often, goals are created by focusing only on the tangible. To have inner-happiness and fulfillment, goals serve us better if we don't neglect the intangible experience.

Awareness #1: Goals and Commitments

We have been taught in North America to apply SMART goals (Specific, Measurable, Attainable, Realistic, Timely/Tangible) which teach us to attain tangible, realistic circumstances which we can measure. When we base our idea of success on tangible outcomes, it limits our outcome to outer experience, and boxes us in to think we know what we want even before we set our first foot toward doing anything.

'SMART' goals do not allow us to set our sights high. Sometimes we need to set goals that we don't know how we can achieve; it's the experience that is fulfilling, not the result.

The experience of making $75K or $100K may each provide the same experience, but the specific dollar amount attached to that experience limits the feelings of success. Are we less of a person if we make $1000 under an expectation? Are we more of a person if we make $1000 more?

Focusing on the experience and learning potential in life is what will give us true fulfillment.

Achieving a feeling, like that of inner-happiness, which cannot be measured or seen but only felt, is difficult to capture under the SMART goals definition.

SMART goals limit the intangible experiences and cause us to dismiss goals which we cannot see and measure. (Reminder: Specific, Measurable, Attainable, Realistic, Timely/Tangible.)

Setting experiential goals allows for flexibility on the means, and allows more inner-freedom in setting out to achieve it. **There is greater strength in being flexible and bending than in being rigid and breaking.**

When we set experiential goals, we essentially remove the blinders of focusing only on one tangible expectation and leave the mind open to acceptance of 'blessings in disguise' that may occur.

Personal success is always achieved when focusing on creating value instead of just 'what's in it for me'. It allows each of us the privilege of fulfilling a need to contribute to others; a deep spiritual human need of ultimate fulfillment and happiness.

Equating success to the day the goal is achieved is also a mistake that is often made. When we do this we always feel like we are chasing a dream, but never realizing it—think, lose 20 pounds, get married, retire... before we can say we are happy.

So much emphasis and praise is on goals having been achieved—very little on the small steps toward achievement. If you equate success from day one of the journey to the goal, fulfillment and value arrives from that first moment and through the entire experience of working toward the goal.

The journey to the goal is no less important than the final achievement itself.

> *Strive not to be a success, but rather to be of value.*
>
> Albert Einstein

Identify all the W's (and an H) when establishing goals—who, what, why, when, where, and how. All of these questions are equally important. It is not enough to ask yourself why, but equally important to know what and how.

> Personal example: in setting the goal to write this book, I first limited myself with the statement, 'I want to sell 500,000 copies'. I further impaired my vision when I focused on the money it could bring in—the personal success. Of course, this didn't feel right. My heart knew better, but our indoctrination into the Western World's material/personal gain is firmly set inside each of us.
>
> The goal felt empty. I immediately recognized that, after all, that's not why I was writing the book.
>
> What made the goal really fulfilling was when I changed it to 'write a book that is so compelling and so outstanding that as a result it creates value for 500,000 people'.

I brought the control back to me. I didn't just want to write any book. I wanted to write a book that I thought was so outstanding that 500,000 people would find value and life-changing information within it.

The goal of writing a book became about the quality and not the quantity. What this means to me is that, even if I only sold one book, it would be worth it because, to me, it would be wholly fulfilling to have written a book that was, in my opinion, my best work, **and** that it created value for one other person.

THE GOALS WITHIN YOU

Do you have any goals? If so, here is a great test to determine the quality of your goals. Rank each area of your life, on a scale of 1-10, of how happy you were 5 years ago and how happy you currently are (1-unhappy, 10-happy). Next, determine how you want to be in 1-5 years. Describe what you specifically want to experience in each area that is within your control:

	5 yrs ago	Current Day	In 1-5 yrs
Need for certainty	_____	_____	_____
Need for Love	_____	_____	_____
Need for Variety	_____	_____	_____
Need for Significance	_____	_____	_____
Need for Growth	_____	_____	_____
Need for Contribution	_____	_____	_____
Need for Health	_____	_____	_____
Need for Wealth	_____	_____	_____
Need for Relationships	_____	_____	_____

Not so easy, right? And that's why people put off doing it.

It's easy to say what we don't want. It's better to focus on what we do want. Look at your numbers. Be real. Be thoughtful. Be proud of how far you have come. Be aware if certain areas show a dip. Be bold—never be afraid of putting an 11.

Quick exercises to explain the power of focus.
1. Please **don't** think about football. I said please, but did your mind still picture football?
2. Take a moment, look around the room, and identify everything red. Now, closing your eyes, recall everything you saw that was yellow.

The mind goes where we focus.

We need to have specific goals/experiences/desires to look forward to and work toward to feel happy. Focus the mind on what you want.

Once you've looked at your happiness past and present, and marked up your future, go for it and set some goals in those categories. Basically, make a list. It's that simple (at first). Then, once you have that list, take some time to ask these questions about each of your goals:

1. What would you do if you could do anything you wanted, with no strings attached and no fears?
2. If a genie could grant you three wishes to make you happy, what would you want?
3. Am I only focusing on one area of my life, or do I have goals for all areas of my life?
4. What do I ultimately desire? What do I want to experience?
5. Is the goal within my own control?
6. Why do I want this goal?
7. How can I set out to achieve my goal?

Awareness #1: Goals and Commitments

8. What experience and needs does it fulfill (love, certainty, variety, significance, growth, contribution)?
9. What is my purpose for my goal?
10. Will achieving this goal allow me to help others?
11. What fears or obstacles stand between me and my goal? How can I address those fears and obstacles? How do those fears and obstacles affect me? What am I willing to do differently if I reach another road block?

Now choose one of your goals and write out three mini-goals that can help achieve your big goal. For the first mini-goal toward your larger goal, write out three actions you can take to advance toward it.

Another thing I've noticed over the years is that, every time I ask people to rank what they want their life to be in 1-5 years, they **never put 10**. I find it crazy that we are afraid to put 10 down because we think perfection is impossible, or that we don't want to set ourselves up for failure.

This exercise is not about perfection and failure. It's about stretching yourself to attain what you want. Don't shy away from the 10's. You deserve them, and you get to choose what 10 looks like. No one else decides.

A good idea is to start a commitment journal—filled in weekly—to help you keep working toward one or more goals. Ask yourself: "What can I commit to this week in order to work toward my goal."

Keep yourself accountable.

> *You want to know the biggest illusion about success? That it's like a pinnacle to be climbed, a thing to be possessed, or a static result to be achieved. If you want to succeed, if you want to achieve all your outcomes, you have to think of success as a process, a way of life, a habit of mind, a strategy for life.*
>
> Tony Robbins

We don't have to be perfect to deserve our goals. We don't have to be perfect to be phenomenal. We just have to want it and work for it. Let's not get attached to the story of selling ourselves short. Let's not come to the table with past assumptions. We are enough. Right now. Right here. We can learn how to align ourselves with amazing intentions (remember, you can put an 11), and detach ourselves from expectations and fixed mindsets.

If you have a weakness, address it. Don't let shortcomings be your excuse. If you have a goal to be a great motivational speaker, but have a fear of public speaking, join Toastmasters. Figure out how to address the weakness or any roadblocks. **Do not accommodate the fear by adapting the goal to it.**

When we become attached to a fixed, expected outcome, we attach ourselves to a future identity of self. This creates a void within our being because we think that we are never good enough, and that our current self is neither deserving nor adequate. We become so focused on our fixed outcome that we begin to lose the joy of what we are already experiencing, because we discount it. We don't appreciate that what we are learning and experiencing is what we need for our higher good, as opposed to what we want.

Most of us set goals typically based on our wants as opposed to our needs. The pain we feel as a result of the discomfort of not being good enough, or failing to meet that goal, is the universe's way of reminding us to be present, grateful and joyful of the journey, not just the destination. Set goals, being mindful of what is needed to feel fulfilled, as opposed to what we think will make us happy on the outside.

When we set goals and embark on them with a fixed mindset attached to an expected outcome, we set ourselves up for feelings of failure and inadequacy, ultimately resulting in unhappiness.

When we live with the courage to take on a growth mindset, in which we continuously grow and learn, we open ourselves up to an internal fulfillment that is long lasting. When we let go of expectations and fixed outcomes, we appreciate the acceptance of getting what we need as opposed to what we want. We begin to see more clearly and feel more joy with the obstruction of fear and discomfort removed.

Trust, have faith, do what 'feels' right rather than what we 'think' is right.

> *When you dance, your purpose is not to get to a certain place on the floor. It's to enjoy each step along the way.*
>
> Wayne Dyer

Awareness #2: Passion And Purpose

What is the meaning of our existence?

In Bronnie Ware's *The Top 5 Regrets of the Dying*, the palliative carer penned the most common regrets from patients.

1. I wish I'd had the courage to live a life true to myself, not the life others expected of me.
2. I wish I hadn't worked so hard.
3. I wish I'd had the courage to express my feelings.
4. I wish I had stayed in touch with my friends.
5. I wish that I had let myself be happier.

One certainty we all have is, given we were born, we will die. What is uncertain is how we spend our time between the two. Living without a passion and a purpose is living like you are waiting to die.

Passion is our fire. Purpose is our journey to share that fire with the rest of the world.

We each have a passion and purpose, and we possess many gifts; we just need to figure it all out. The figuring it out part is the adventure of a lifetime; don't be afraid to go on a quest, to explore, and to express your uniqueness. Fear not the road less travelled. Carve out a new path. Hiding from who we truly are results in a poor quality of life.

- For some people, right from the time they are children, they know what their passion and purpose is, and they go for it.

Awareness #2: Passion and Purpose

- For others there is a deep-down knowing of their passion and purpose, but the cost of pursuing the realness of it seems too high. They don't go for it.
- Then there are those for whom identification of a passion and purpose is difficult. They may agonize and give up, or they might commit to researching until they find their gold at the end of the rainbow.

The important thing is, let go of the artificial stimulants that are stifling your search, stealing your natural energy. Don't settle. Passion left undiscovered—unpursued—creates a void which cannot be filled with food, overspending, drink, or other artificial 'fillers'.

If you don't know what your passion is, realize that one reason for your existence on earth is to find it.

Oprah Winfrey

Make it your life mission to find your purpose and live purposefully; anything less is unnatural.

How do you know if you've found your passion and purpose?

You love and look forward to doing it even if you don't get paid.

Some think others are 'lucky' to find passion and purpose, but it's not like a lottery; it's hard work and searching and introspection.

Luck is preparation meeting opportunity.

Finding your passion is like finding your soul mate. People will ask, "How did you know 'he' was the one?" The answer is, "I just knew."

You know you have found your passion and purpose if it is something that you have to do, could not live without, cannot imagine living without it, and do it regardless of monetary reward. If your soul speaks to you and that message is heard, and makes you smile and fills your heart, then you have found your passion. The reason most people do not figure out their passion or their purpose is because they let fear overpower, or they just stop experiencing new things. They settle.

If you are unsure of what your passion is—have not found it—do not give up looking. Participate in things that interest you, and involve yourself in activities you have never tried. **The key is to follow your intuition.** Talk to others about how they feel about you. Take note of the common ground that surfaces in how you want to feel, and how you do feel, when you are doing certain things or are around certain people or places.

The best place to begin your quest is looking through your past. What did you love to do as a child or young adult? What principles do you stand for? What excites you and puts a smile on your face when you think about it? What hardship did you endure in your past and have worked to overcome? How can you help others overcome that similar struggle?

> *More and more, a psychiatrist is approached today by patients who confront him with human problems rather than neurotic symptoms. Some of the people who nowadays call on a psychiatrist would have seen a pastor, priest or rabbi in former days. Now they often refuse to be handed over to a clergyman and instead confront the doctor with questions such as, 'What is the meaning of my life?'*
>
> Viktor E. Frankl, M.D., Ph.D.

Living in a technologically advanced world of busy-ness and disconnection, we often seek medical advice and intervention for negative feelings such as depression and anxiety. These feelings are a normal part of human experience and are signs from the body that there is a void within our lives. These feelings are not meant to be detached from our being, but rather an indication to seek solutions.

These are moments when we may need to seek life advice.

Psychologist Viktor E. Frankl prescribed his patients suffering with emotions such as despair, grief, and depression with something called logotherapy. It challenges people to confront and reorient themselves toward the meaning of their life. It's not just about getting a person to say things that are difficult or disagreeable to say, but hearing things that are difficult and disagreeable to hear about oneself.

Hearing someone question or challenge our meaning of life may sound easy on paper. Questioning our purpose and our beliefs can shake us to the core. It forces us to question our identity and our existence. This makes us feel uncomfortable; it's human nature to resist feeling uncomfortable. The state of discomfort—the resistance—puts us in murky waters.

If we are suffering, due to a lack of meaning, there is only one thing that can change and relieve the suffering—a shift in perspective and attitude.

Happiness arises from balance and meaning in our life. Balance comes from aligning our influences, beliefs, emotions, and actions with meaning in our life. When balance is combined with meaning, the result is fulfillment and happiness.

Upon studying many people who suffer with mental anguish, the only thing that changed from one moment to the next was that a new thought they registered freed them of their suffering; a thought that provided them with meaning about why they were suffering.

Changing our environment or physical state will not solve a problem of the mind. Mind problems are properly solved with changes of the mental state.

Finding our purpose is a primary motivation in life which can only be fulfilled by the individual on her own. No one can do it for anyone else. If left unexplored, lack of purpose can cause an 'existential vacuum'—a void which begs to be constantly filled.

To affirm this, A National Institute of Mental Health study echoes others in concluding that 16% of the people who participated said that making a lot of money was considered very important, but a whopping 78% answered that finding a meaning and purpose to their life was very important.

This vacuum manifests as boredom. Many see boredom as a negative feeling in which to escape and seek excitement. Boredom is our call to action, our essential need to find meaning in our life; to ask ourselves why we exist and why we wake up each morning.

When we are uncertain, either by lack of instinct or education, we fill this void by doing what others do, or what they tell us to do. We end up living someone else's life.

With a growing void we reach to artificial means such as food, money, drugs, power, consumerism.

Purpose differs from person to person, and each of us is responsible to determine what our purpose is. It is only through living the steps of a disciplined life of doing what is not necessarily easiest, but is in our best interest, that we find fulfillment. This may mean we may have to make choices that are inconvenient, not easy, or difficult. The great thing is: the results of these somewhat tough choices align with our true essence—the path to collateral happiness.

In pursuit of our purpose, we discover who we are and what we are made of (self-actualization), and we overcome limitations (self-transcendence).

Just as self-actualization is not an object of intention or an attainable aim, neither is happiness. Happiness is the result of surrendering to discipline and commitment. The commitment to learn how to love oneself.

Once we love our self we can begin to spread our wings and open ourselves up to complete connection with others and the world.

Edith Weisskopf-Joelson, professor of psychology at the University of Georgia, contended the current philosophy that unhappiness is a symptom of the failure to meet social or cultural expectations. She argued that this value system of unavoidable unhappiness is increased by unhappiness of being unhappy. If people were given opportunity to be proud of their suffering and consider it 'ennobling rather than degrading', then we could relinquish shame associated with being unhappy.

In finding the purpose of our life, pain is unavoidable. Recognize this concept, then celebrate and revere that act of recognition. We are called to action through 'struggle' as a biological requirement for growth; something we can lean into and not run from.

To bring increased clarity to the meaning in our lives, look through a positive lens: one in which we reflect with pride and joy on all the lessons brought forth from struggles.

To be free and happy is not liberty from limitations, but liberty on how we address those limitations.

Think of discomfort/change (to be made to reach goals) as a swamp that stands between you and your purpose. You have to struggle through to get to the other side. If you are like many, you might not even be able to see what your purpose is, or what you are working toward, until you actually cross the swamp.

If we can't see the prize, we tend to think we should avoid the swamp because it's not worth it. We can find a guide to help navigate, but we still have to take each step.

So, for all seeking to figure out or uncover your life purpose, know that it might not be a straight line. We may only see the next step, not all steps, nor the final step. The dots might not connect until the final puzzle piece is placed. The journey to purpose will be unique; lots of ups and downs and side to sides.

- Put yourself out there and start experiencing new things.
- Be 'out'-standing in the crowd.
- Get it wrong. (Don't be afraid to get it wrong.)
- Take as long as you need.
- Let it take unique shape.
- Keep going.
- Get some great hip-waders and cross that swamp.

> *It's better to live your own life imperfectly than to imitate someone else's perfectly.*
> — Elizabeth Gilbert

Do model success of others. Use it as a mirror, not a Xerox machine.

Awareness #3: Identifying Core Values

Unless we spend time working on self-discovery and self-awareness, we cannot answer the question, 'who am I?'

Many will answer this question with their job title or profession; this because they aren't sure how else to answer. But a job title or a profession is what we do, not who we are.

It's common for people to believe they are products of their past experiences, a consequence of what life has thrown at them.

To reflect on the past, reassess life, and determine who we want to be, is key to inner-happiness. Often, we feel powerless in deciding who we are because we believe it's already been decided.

Assumptions are one of life's great mistakes.

We are creatures who are well practiced in making simple concepts complex. We can change who we want to be at any moment in our life: we simply need to choose.

One path of action to determine the 'who you are' is to spend a few minutes reading the following table of attributes and qualities. Add some to the existing list if you like.

List your top 5 core values:

1. _____
2. _____
3. _____
4. _____
5. _____

ATTRIBUTES AND QUALITIES

Accountability	Diligence	Hope
Accuracy	Disciplined	Humility
Action	Dynamic	Humour
Adaptability	Eco-conscious	Imagination
Adventure	Easy-going	Impartiality
Affection	Education	Independence
Affordability	Effectiveness	Initiator
Alertness	Emotional	Innovation
Alternative	Empathetic	Inspiring
Ambition	Empowering	Integrity
Assertiveness	Energy	Intelligence
Attentive	Engaging	Joyfulness
Authenticity	Enjoyment	Kindness
Balance	Enterprising	Knowledge
Beauty	Enthusiasm	Leadership
Boldness	Equality	Learning
Broadmindedness	Ethical	Listening
Calm	Excellence	Love
Career	Exclusivity	Loyalty
Cleanliness	Expressive	Luxury
Clear-thinking	Faith	Maturity
Collaborative	Fair	Method
Cool	Facilitation	Meticulous
Comfort	Family	Modesty
Commitment	Fashion	Natural
Community	Fitness	Networking
Communication	Flexibility	Nurturing
Compassion	Focus	Objectivity
Competence	Forgiveness	Optimism
Confidence	Freedom	Organization
Conscientious	Friendliness	Originality
Considerate	Fulfillment	Passion
Consistent	Fun	Patience
Conservative	Gentleness	Peace
Contribution	Generosity	Perfection
Cooperation	Growth	Perseverance
Courage	Happiness	Persistence
Creativity	Health	Planning
Customer delight	Helpful	Playfulness
Dependability	Honorable	Pleasant
Determination	Honesty	Polite

Awareness #3: Identifying Core Values

Positivity	Self-control	Tenacious
Possessions	Self-awareness	Thankfulness
Possessive	Sensibility	Thoroughness
Practical	Sensitivity	Tolerance
Proactive	Service	Trustworthiness
Productive	Sexiness	Understanding
Professionalism	Sincerity	Uniqueness
Prosperity	Simplicity	Value
Purposefulness	Sociability	Versatility
Precision	Speed	Victory
Punctuality	Specialness	Vintage
Quality	Spiritual	Visionary
Realism	Spontaneous	Warmth
Reliability	Stable	Willpower
Resourcefulness	Supportive	Wisdom
Respect	Strength	Youthfulness
Responsibility	Tact	Zeal
Safety	Talent	
Security	Teamwork	

PRACTICAL PRACTICE

Once you've done that, choose the five most important—those essential for your peace of mind and survival.

What are those five (in the now) attributes and qualities?

If you are uncertain, ask yourself, "what situations in life irritate and make me angry?"

Anger is a sign one of your values is being violated. It means there is a value that is core to your authentic self which you are willing to stand up for, no matter what.

When you feel certain about your top five, ask yourself:

"Do these qualities represent who I want to be, or are they representative of whom I've always been?"

Take time to think about goals you have: personal and professional—will you be able to achieve your current goals with these five values backing you/representing you?

For example, if you did not put health on your list, do you need to consider adding it in order to meet your health goals?

Reassess or reprioritize if there are conflicts with who you were and who you want to be. This is an opportunity to let go of the past and move forward.

Picture the 'you' who has been hiding inside yourself. Envision the natural being that does not need artificial happiness.

Redo the list while thinking about 'who' you want to become.

The next part is to ask yourself the question, what do I need in order to feel _____(insert value). Then expand on it.

For example:

What do I need in order to feel... 'authenticity'?

Expanded example:
I, 'Linda', feel authentic when I... um... when I allow myself to be true to my feelings, like when I respect myself the way I respect others. When I honour my opinion over the opinions of others. When I feel a celebration inside me for having been independent and confident about how I presented myself in a situation.

I feel authentic—the real deal—when I don't go along with ideas I don't support. When I stand up for certain ethical beliefs. When I say no to a glass of wine (because I just don't want one, but there's peer pressure). When I say no to various family commitments (because I simply want to take an afternoon off and rest).

I'm my true self when I'm not judging others' motives. When I don't worry about what people think about my clothing choices.

Awareness #3: Identifying Core Values

So, what I need to be authentic is to remember that I have great ideas, am a good listener, and a decent decider.

I need to remember that I dress to please me. That I support causes that are close to my heart. I need to celebrate my decisions. That each of us is unique and that's a gift. I need to look in the mirror and totally tell myself I rock.

Stating what you need in this manner allows you to take control of your own life instead of limiting your happiness to the control of everyone around you.

Many say they feel loved when someone comes up and hugs them. But that limitation puts the 'loved feeling' under the control of someone else. Not that there's anything wrong with a wonderful, warm hug. The key to owning your feelings is to feel your lovability when you are hugged, and place it back in your court, to feel the love inside you when you hug back, or initiate a hug yourself rather than waiting for it.

The importance of knowing our values helps us solidify our decisions. By asking ourselves how the solution aligns with our values, then answering, we will know exactly what we need to do.

For example, if we ask ourselves, "Should I take this job?" "Should I stay married to this person?"…

…If the people or situation align with your values then, yes. If they do not align, then ask, "Am I willing to sacrifice my happiness?" "Am I willing to tolerate a violation of my core value?" You don't have to 'should' anything. You choose.
When we live in violation of our core values we cannot experience inner-happiness. Knowing our values is key to understanding who we are and what decisions we need to make.

Living in alignment with our values brings inner-happiness, creating collateral happiness.

Awareness #4: Scheduling and Prioritizing

A BIG ASK

Shift your priorities by putting you first, family second, and work third.

That's right. It may seem impossible. The concept might sound ridiculous. But ask yourself this: how long until you burn out when you put career and family first? Notice, 'when', not 'if'.

Who will you be good for at that point? What are you really trying to prove to yourself?

How to shift your priorities:

- Use a weekly planning calendar/a blank book—whatever suits you.
- Schedule in your bedtime for each day.
- Then fill in your meditation/downtime/learning time.
- Mark up the times you'll eat.
- Do the same with the timeslots you'll engage in movement.
- Add in a 'date' with yourself or significant other.
- Pop in one with a friend/or family.
- Finally, schedule your extras and your work.

It may seem crazy, but can you see how you've opened up your schedule, and how it can all fit?

Scheduling eventually becomes a habit in which you place yourself at the front of the line. When you are available for yourself first,

Awareness #4: Scheduling and Prioritizing

you can participate in all other activities and relationships from a place of wellness and wholeness. Yes, it may seem overwhelming at first, and feel foreign, but those who live life with this priority system are those who thrive.

The key is to begin with a list and a calendar. If you can't fill in the times in a calendar, at least start with a task list. For example:

Monday
1. Make food plan and prep any meals
2. Workout/yoga
3. Get dressed
4. Gratitude journal
5. Emails, phone calls, schedule dates (friends, self, spouse, business, fun time such as wine or cooking class)
6. Eat something healthy
7. Professional Work
8. Housework (laundry, cleaning)
9. Meditation
10. Read/watch a video

It is extremely empowering to take control of your life, and choose to be who you want to be, without feeling guilty about it. It is liberating.

> *To live a more balanced existence, you have to recognize that not doing everything that comes along is okay. There's no need to overextend yourself. All it takes is realizing that it's all right to say no when necessary and then focus on your highest priorities.*
>
> Stephen R. Covey, author
> *7 Habits of Highly Successful People*

It's essential to know who you are, and what you want, so you can start to align your time with your desires. Once you start to do this, you will find yourself leading a happier and more fulfilling life.

What are your priorities today? Do they align with your values and your goals? If not, reassess and shift your priorities so that they are in alignment. Schedule your needs first. For those who hold jobs, is dedicating your life to work, and helping someone else make money, more important than your own health and your own life? How can it be a win/win? What needs to change in order for you to thrive, and to balance various aspects of your life? What must go? What can stay? What can be redesigned? What are you willing to sacrifice? What are you not willing to sacrifice? What can you delegate? Who can you ask for help? What are your ABC's—your priorities?

Deborah Adele, author of *The Yamas and Niyamas,* said that balance is like this. Spreading ourselves thin looks impressive, but in the end we are the first to lose. The health and wellbeing of our body, mind and spirit is a powerful resource and, by keeping ourselves in balance, we can stride through life with greater competence and ease.

Awareness #5: Self-Limiting Beliefs

The number one predictor of success is your belief in yourself. A belief is nothing more than a feeling of certainty. By being aware of the limiting beliefs we hold, we can change them.

Whether you think you can, or you think you can't— you're right.

Henry Ford

We can all be game-changers.

Our beliefs, which form our preferences, dislikes, fears, and rules, are created by external influences from the day we are born. They are formulated in our mind in accordance to the law of patterns. Beliefs can either limit or grow us. Self-limiting beliefs that become ingrained block our authentic self from shining through. It is critical to release these beliefs in order to allow our authentic selves to thrive. Since the mind groups thoughts into patterns, we often link past occurrences with future results. Doing this creates illusion.

Self-limiting beliefs are recognized by identifying disharmony in life. Most of us have conditioned our minds to blame something outside of us when disharmony arises.

Anthony de Mello states, "We are happy when people/things conform and unhappy when they don't. People and events don't disappoint us, our models of reality do. It is my model of reality that determines my happiness or disappointment."

He's right. Most of us fight to justify our system rather than re-examine the belief that holds us a prisoner of the disharmony.

Holding on to negative self-limiting beliefs prevents us from experiencing our true essence.

Limiting beliefs can potentially manifest in the following ways:
- When you make excuses or blame others.
- When you complain about things.
- When you indulge in negative thoughts or habits.
- When you talk to yourself in negative ways.
- When you jump to conclusions and/or make assumptions.
- When you hesitate to express your fears.
- When you worry about failure or about making mistakes.
- When you think about procrastinating.
- When you think how to be perfect.

Often it is our belief system of 'should' that is the very thing which hinders our creation of inner-happiness. When beliefs become subconscious, we stop questioning their validity because we think we 'know.' Forever keep the door open to learning, questioning, and reflection. If we don't (keep that door open/stay alert/be aware), it becomes difficult, if not impossible, to recognize a flawed belief.

In order to let go of self-limiting beliefs, acknowledge what illusions we ascribe to.

One of the biggest illusions in life is that we must feel good in order to take action.

Did you feel good when you were challenged by some of the advice in this book? Do you ever feel like working out?

Of course not. It's a certainty you've felt uncomfortable, scared, pained, frustrated. And, over time: hopeful, driven, excited and eager.

Awareness #5: Self-Limiting Beliefs

I am not what happened to me, I am what I choose to become.

C. G. Jung

One way to find self-limiting beliefs and illusions, that we are not aware of, is to ask the following questions, the answers to which quickly identify a belief ingrained in you since childhood.

These profound questions help drill down on unconscious patterns we fall into, and need to change in order to take control of our lives.

As a child, whose love did you crave the most? (Mom, Dad, friend, biological parent, adopted parent, aunt, uncle, grandparent...)

Why did you crave their love?

How did you feel you had to be as a result? What belief and behavior did you develop due to this?

How did/can this experience make you a stronger and better person?

If you didn't crave love and attention, was it because it was readily given to you?

Do you now expect others to give love and attention to you, without anything in return, because it has become your expectation?

What can you learn from this experience to make you a better person?

Sit with these questions a bit.

Deep Jane, Deep

The walking had turned to jogging had turned to an even-paced run—whatever it was called, it had turned on a switch inside me.

I became more aware of everything, which was overwhelming.

A lot of the overwhelming was as magical as the process of how chia jam sort of makes itself overnight.

Some of the awareness was that I knew I wasn't watching as much television. I was eating, not perfectly, but leaps and bounds more healthily than I had in the past. I made time to write in my gratitude journal.

But some of that status-overwhelm was negative—like whining to my girlfriend about my relationship with Jack. When I complained about him I felt pained inside. When I waxed nostalgic, paging through old photos on a flash drive, I ached for the Jack I once knew to return. I'd pictured it as a bit of a Knight in shining armour moment, except he wore a sexy all-weather high-visibility running jacket—green to match his eyes.

Looking at old pictures made me bawl my head off. And, while I sobbed into the cushions of the sofa, I thought of his distancing himself from me, the fact he does not help—when was the last time he did a load of laundry? Okay, he took care of the lawn or paid the neighbour's son to. I crashed when I tried to remember when he'd last tucked the kids in. I damned his friends, Michael and Jason, who could get him to do anything and go anywhere with one text.

By the time I convinced myself he was filing for divorce, I was in the bathroom, splashing cool water on my puffy eyes. The mirror image didn't help.

I wasn't prepared for the truth, (at least the way I perceived it). Jack didn't love me.

What I didn't know is that I'd blurt that out when I saw Grace. I hadn't even said 'hi'. I walked into her office, sat down and said, "He doesn't love me."

My eyes were still sore from crying, but it didn't stop me from starting up again.

"What do you need in order to feel loved?" A tissue reached my hand.

Grace was almost too patient. She should be telling me he was a son of a bitch and I'd chosen the wrong man. Inside I was all "why did I start this coaching?" But when I thought that, my feet tingled. And when I looked down at them I saw a nice pair of legs and thighs, and I scooched my butt in the chair and realized I wasn't filling the whole seat. I was wearing a skort. Before this morning I hadn't even known I owned a skort.

"Can you think of when things started shifting between the two of you? When you started to withdraw your love from him?" asked Grace.

Withdraw from him? Was she kidding?

Maybe other clients could understand and answer her question, but I couldn't comprehend it. I was a loser.

"Things happen over time," she said. "A seed is planted and a tree grows. We are happy with ourselves, confident enough to enjoy time with others, loving ourselves without knowing that's what it is—self-love—and attracting great things. A career, a running partner who becomes a husband—carefree, childless, and fresh, we are fulfilled. But, little by little, we are overcome with life, good things that demand time and energy. Amazing things that, nevertheless, need prioritizing. All of a sudden we are overfilled. Shortcuts are taken in self-care. We place ourselves at the bottom of the list. We put ourselves after diapers, even after scrubbing toilets."

I blew my nose. My breathing had evened.

What I learned was that, over time, I had stopped loving me and had begun to withdraw from him. I had been expecting him to save me, to pick up the pieces of a broken me and glue them back together; to initiate a new relationship.

There was serious introspection: I wondered if I had ever loved myself fully. And, if I couldn't completely love myself, why was I expecting Jack to love me.

Since I'd started 'movement' I'd felt energized. I wondered if I had the energy to change him. My new energy was making me question things again rather than take life as status quo, but how could that relate to my crumbling marriage?

And, of course, I blurted that out that question. "How can I change him?"

There might as well have been a game show 'wrong' buzzer.

MUURRP.

But on the way to chastising myself about not being smart, I realized I knew the right answer. Deep inside I knew.

Grace didn't let it go. "Him?" she asked.

"I meant me." I said.

And I did. I did mean me. I just didn't want to admit it. Nor did I want to change.

"What do I have to change to change me so that I completely love myself and become lovable?"

We talked about how it is hard for others to love us when we don't love ourselves. How inaccessible we make ourselves.

Whether I scheduled a date night, or he did, didn't matter—it mattered that we go on a date. I understood it, but I fought that feeling. I wanted that Knight in shining armour to sweep me off my feet, like in an epic romance movie.

It wasn't until I literally hit the sidewalk a block from Grace's office, stumbling on an offset paving stone, that I got that I could and would sweep myself off my own feet. I sat on the sidewalk—people probably thought me wacky.

The outdoors and movement had begun to transform me, but there was still a lot of inside work to do.

I sat on the sidewalk and thought back to some of Grace's words: "We as women need to let go that the man always needs to initiate in order for it to 'count'. Or that they need to read our minds. We can change that rule too. We can choose how we want to be loved."

"How does Jack even know what's going on inside me?" I asked the street.

"Can I help you?" said a forty-possibly-fifty-something woman holding a large designer purse. She reached down a bejeweled hand to help me up. I glimpsed lacy underwear under her skirt as she bent to grasp my elbow. I wondered for a second if my Superbuy-discount underwear was showing before remembering I was wearing a skort.

"Our brains do not think the same as each other, therefore creating limited rules where we decide our loved ones are supposed to 'just know' is a dangerous mindset. Asking for help is courage not weakness," I said.

She released me. "Erm, I just wanted to know if you wanted helping up. Maybe you are concussed. Your knee is bleeding," said the Amazonian glamour queen.

"Collateral damage," I said as she backed away.

I was deep into epiphany by the time she'd quick-stepped to the end of the block. I thought about my mother, Jack, my negative neighbour, my fear of honesty with my girls-night-out friends.

Amazon goddess was crossing the street, cellphone to her ear. Probably calling an ambulance or the police.

Internally I had a conversation with myself: I need to figure out what I need to feel loved and determine how I can control it. Fill my own needs, my own love bucket, then my husband's. Maybe if I start to fill his love bucket, he will fill mine? Maybe if I tell him what I need, he won't have to guess and get it wrong every time? Maybe we need to get back to dating instead of just being roommates?

Amazon goddess watched me from a distance; phone still at her ear. But I finished the conversation with myself before I high-tailed it out of there.

"I need to create a positive relationship with myself, love myself, before my other relationships will flourish. But how do I do that?" I asked my bloody knee.

"You will call upon Grace for that," it answered.

Awareness #6: Pain and Pleasure

Complacency breeds stagnation.
Tony Robbins

Most of us do not make changes unless we are inspired or desperate enough to have to make changes. Everything else in-between is comfortable and easy and so we settle for that.

Settling leads to stagnation, like an apple sitting on the counter for weeks. Looks good on the outside, but is slowly rotting away on the inside.

People avoid change, despite the fact they know they want to change, because they associate a great deal of pain with the change. The idea of pain paralyzes them from moving forward.

Focusing on the desired outcome and thinking about the pleasure associated with that outcome is only helpful when followed by action. Procrastination occurs because we associate pain, rather than pleasure, with the task we put off.

If we want to change a bad habit that is associated with pleasure, such as overeating ice cream to soothe self-pity, then we will need to find a way to associate pain with ice cream and find a positive new habit to replace the old one. This can be challenging, and is why breaking old, negative habits can be difficult. Who doesn't want to enjoy ice cream and be pleasured by the taste? We have to break the negative thought association attached to the habit, retrain the mind, and repeat the new habit consistently over time.

One of the ways to overcome the pain-pleasure battle is to ask: "What will this 'cost' me if I don't change?"

We forget to look at what will happen if we don't change. When we do look at what we will be missing, the idea of change can become intriguing, exciting, and seem so much more doable. And, because we haven't all developed putting ourselves first, sometimes that change can be absolutely 'charged, motivated, driven' by how change will impact those who are most important to us.

To succeed, we need pain to push us and pleasure to pull us. As humans we tend to move from pain to pleasure. This means if we use pain to push us but do not have a pleasure to pull us, the moment we stop feeling pain, we stop doing what we were doing. It is important to have both a pain to push us and a pleasure to pull us. We can learn to teach ourselves to think in long term results or outcomes rather than on instant gratification of desires.

PRACTICAL PRACTICE

What situations in your life have been worth the 'struggle', and have felt as if pleasure was pulling you toward the goal?

Identify the pleasure-pull in any new habits you have begun to establish since beginning this book. Can you break down the ongoing work into manageable bytes in order to feel the pleasure-pull more often?

Awareness #7: Metaprograms

What are they?

Mental processes.

They are like programs, and are the ways that we process information and internalize patterns that drive our behaviour and influence the way we function. Metaprograms are ways we can engage others for a variety of goal-related reasons. We use metaprograms to help us sort through and decide which information to pay attention to since the conscious mind can only take in so much at a time.

The path to becoming a great communicator and reducing misunderstandings is through metaprograms. **If we want to have love and connection with other human beings for our fulfillment, we will need to know how to communicate with other human beings.** Metaprograms are a great communication tool to help identify what motivates and discourages people.

Taking the time to learn about metaprograms helps us to become aware of the vast differences in how people react to the same thing. For example, you give a speech at work and half the staff respond well, while the other is bored or frustrated. You begin to wonder if there is something wrong with you and why you can only connect with half your team.

Knowing the different ways people think and respond can be extremely beneficial to your inner-happiness. You start to see it really isn't just you, but in fact how you are communicating with others that is the concern. Improving communication and understanding your own metaprograms can play a big part in creating

Collateral Happiness: The Power Behind the Facade

collateral happiness because, once you understand how to communicate effectively, it can bring a big relief to frustration, and ease internal tension.

You could have the most amazing idea at work, but if you aren't presenting it in a way that people can appreciate and understand, that idea will be a flop (and that can lead to extreme unhappiness for you).

You may think you failed and begin to question your material when, in fact, it might not have been the material that was the problem, but how you communicated it. Many people become frustrated at work and feel like a failure. It's not **what** you said, but **how** you said it, that made all the difference.

When it comes to understanding how people process information, there are seven metaprograms as described in Tony Robbins' work, *Unlimited Power*.

The **first** metaprogram involves knowing if people are inspired to move toward pleasure or are influenced to move away from pain. For example, if someone wants a higher level of fitness, and states "I want to work out to become fit," that is a 'moving toward' metaprogram.

Whereas, I don't want to become a couch potato, is a 'moving away' metaprogram, or process.

Each process can produce the result of fitness.
- I want to work out to become fit. (Moving toward type of metaprogram)
- I don't want to become a couch potato. (Moving away type of metaprogram).

Each is as effective, depending on the type of person who is looking to be fitter.

We are each wired differently. The way we approach targets and goals is dependent on how we think. Some of us are motivated by the carrot, others by the stick. Notice how people talk to you. Do they state what they want or what they don't want? That may give you a better indication of how to communicate with that person.

The **second** metaprogram involves knowing if people deal with external or internal frames of references. Do they need to hear praise or do they need to praise themselves? You can ask someone what they think of a job they did. Do they make a reference about what everyone else thought? Or, do they focus on their own strengths and weaknesses and not care what everyone else does or says?

The **third** metaprogram involves knowing whether people are concerned by what's in it for them personally or what's in it for them and other people. Some people like to help other people while others like to help themselves. Neither is good or bad; it is merely how people think.

The **fourth** metaprogram involves how we sort information by similarities or differences. Some people group information by what is the same or common. Others only see the differences and the exceptions. Both types of people can see the same picture yet give you different explanations of what they see.

The **fifth** metaprogram involves determining how someone processes information in order to be convinced. First we need to determine if someone is a visual, auditory or kinesthetic learner. Do they need to see it, hear it or experience it? Then we ask: how often do they need to be convinced? Once, twice, over a period of time, or consistently forever? Some people need lots of confirmation or verification, while others only need it once or twice.

The **sixth** metaprogram involves whether decisions are made out of necessity or possibility. Some people make decisions based on doing something because they have to, and to feel safe and secure. Others make decisions because they want to, and like the possibility of the unknown—of what may evolve.

The **seventh** metaprogram involves knowing how people like to work. Do they like to work independently, cooperatively with others, or with others as long as they have the sole responsibility of the task? Some people want to be a part of a group, others want to be alone. If we know how co-workers or our kids like to work, we can be much more respectful to allow people to be their best. It reduces frustration and anxiety.

We do not all think and process the same.

Once we combine different personality types (look up DISC or Myers Briggs) with differences in the way we process information, and add on top of it male and female dissimilarities, it becomes a breeding ground for conflict which can lead to unhappiness. Knowing this can help us appreciate the differences, allow ourselves to be different, to stand out from the crowd, and to respect others while they do what they do best.

No one is right or wrong. We are all entitled to our own opinions and feelings. We simply need to understand and appreciate it. We also need to learn how to explore common ground and be respectful of boundaries—our own and those of others.

Communication: it is also helpful to remember that none of us are mind readers. If something is bothering or concerning us, it's necessary to find the confidence and courage to let other people know what we are thinking. We have to be okay asking for help. It's okay to let others do things differently from our way of doing them. There is more than one way to get to the same goal.

Awareness #8: Changing Our Language

Changing our language—the way we speak to ourselves and others—has a huge impact on our lives. Words matter.

Reframing what we perceive as negative events makes a massive difference in how we learn from those events. As well, statements of gratitude build our self-esteem and motivate.
Think about this common statement we say to ourselves: "I am a failure."

This phrase—four words—can change mood, throw us into a negative swirl, wreak consequences of self-hate, and cause over-indulgence.

Restructuring "I am a failure" to "I am learning", is positive and truthful. "I am learning" is not going to take us on a trip to add further insults about our abilities. Restructuring helps us take one step toward positive change.

Dropping negative words such as 'diet', 'should', 'can't', 'if only, 'but', and 'fail' is a great start. They are unproductive words that get in the way of success and accomplishment.

Using the words 'can', 'do', 'learn', 'choose', 'invite', and 'attract' are much more positive.

Work toward going an hour without using a negative word. Ramp it up to a half day. Take an entire day. Work up to a week of eliminating five or six negative words from your vocabulary, and notice the difference. That means in your thoughts, too. The negative energy these words contain affects your body, mind, and spirit. And they keep us focused on the problem and on the past, rather than on a solution and the future.

Awareness #9: Power Of Positive Influence

Nick Vujicic, a powerful motivational speaker, stated this: "Think of the three biggest discouragers in your life... they're not your biggest discouragers. You are."

That statement is so powerful because it is so true. We let the outside negative voices in and it soon begins to take over our own minds. We slowly give up our power and control by succumbing to the voices of everyone else. In the process, these outside voices soon become imbedded as our thoughts and beliefs.
We listen to everyone else's opinion and end up forgetting our own. We are inundated with the echoes of family, friends, acquaintances, strangers, TV, society, cultural norms, music, the news, and then form beliefs from the voices we let in, and start making excuses for why we 'can't' do something. It's my boss, or my kids, or my husband, or the money. We tell ourselves that we can't be happy because it is everyone else's fault.

But, here's the thing: if negative influences result in negative outcomes then the contrary is also true. Positive influences result in positive outcomes.

Imagine a world where, as a kid, other kids didn't bug you because you were different, but instead applauded you for it. Imagine your parents saying to you that you could do whatever you wanted and money was no object. Imagine if the news was filled with positive success stories. Imagine a mentor encouraging you each day, saying to you that you have what it takes. Wouldn't it be much easier to chase your dreams?

That sounds like a great world in which to live—Fantasy Island—but, negative and positive exist as a law of balance, which means we cannot eliminate negative.

Negative experiences drive us.
Positive influences are what guide us.

Instead of making excuses, we need to be conscious of what kind of influences we choose to be surrounded by, and what voices we let in. If we want to be different or create something new, we will have better success if we find people to talk us into it rather than talk us out of it.

If you want to start a new business, don't take advice from someone who likes a 9-5 job. They will talk you out of it. Not to deter you, but to accommodate his or her partialities. Find someone who has a successful business that will talk you into it.

It is important to learn to shut out the negative voices and to listen to the positive ones, including your own voice. We can become our biggest encourager.

So why do we allow the negative voice of reason to overpower our dreams or desires?

We have not learned the skill of how to recognize ego, the voice of survival. Ego serves us to keep us alive. It's essential to learn to differentiate when ego is keeping us alive and when it is preventing us from growing.

How do we recognize ego? According to Dr. Wayne Dyer, we can recognize ego by the following beliefs:

1. I am what I have. My possessions define me.
2. I am what I do. My achievements define me.
3. I am what others think of me. My reputation defines me.
4. I am separate from everyone. My body defines me as alone.
5. I am separate from all that is missing in my life. My life space is disconnected from my desires.
6. I am separate from God. My life depends on God's assessment of my worthiness.

Wayne Dyer stated in his book, *The Power of Intention*, "No matter how hard you try, intention can't be accessed through ego, so take some time to recognize and readjust any or all of the six beliefs. When the supremacy of ego is weakened in your life, you can see intention and maximize your potential."

If we never learned the skill required to know how to deal with ego, we would end up either trying to ignore it or we would find ourselves succumbing to it. Without this skill, we will constantly submit to self-sabotage.

~~~~~

If you want to end self-sabotage, make sure to recognize the voice of ego and then learn the skill required to retrain your brain with positive influences that will help appease ego and convince that part of your brain that you really are safe.

Unless you learn to calm the ego, it will continuously discourage you from taking action and, eventually you will remove yourself from any situation that hints at discomfort—risk—be it physical or mental. It will signal to keep you in the comfort zone.

This is why, no matter how motivated you feel toward achieving a goal, you will keep sabotaging yourself because it is the brain's default to appease ego first.

When we learn to calm the ego—through awareness—instead of submitting to it, we can stand in our authentic self. When the ego is calm there is head-space for risk taking.

We can calm the ego (and end self-sabotage) by filling our minds with positive influences. When we encounter positive people and locate positive resources the negative influences are reduced—we are only battling one dragon rather than twenty.

PRACTICAL PRACTICE

Here are some suggestions to follow if you find yourself in a situation where you need to quiet ego's voice in order to take a risk.

1. Remind yourself that you are in competition with no one. You are not here to impress anyone. You are here to execute your dream.
2. You can do everything in small manageable steps. You don't have to take a running, giant leap.
3. Tell yourself you are more than interested, you are committed.
4. If you stumble, you can change your path, you don't have to change your goal.
5. Remove negative influences and invite in as many positive influences as possible: people, books, videos. Learn from the wisdom of others. Note their mistakes. Model their successes.
6. Remind yourself that failure is learning.
7. Remind yourself of the times you succeeded in the past. Close your eyes and put yourself in the state of mind which you occupied at that time.

If you currently don't have the right influences in your life to help propel you into positive results, get some. This is absolutely necessary. There are tons of positive mentors with great books, quotes, and documentaries. Read them and watch them every day. Bring these people into your life through their words. You don't necessarily need these people in your life in person. Surround yourself with their positive thoughts and beliefs that will inspire you to become better. Use positive influence to inspire you to make great decisions.

A ROUNDUP OF WHAT NOT TO DO AND A REFRAME

☹ Don't surround yourself with those who will hold you back or keep you stagnant.

- ☺ Bring as much positivity into your life as you can, it will directly affect your results by filtering your thoughts, emotions and actions.
- ☹ Don't allow the voice of ego to listen to outside negative voices and overpower your mind.

Remember, we cannot remove the voice of ego, we can learn to quiet its voice to a whisper.

- ☺ Ego does serve a purpose to keep us safe; learn to recognize when it's keeping you from growing.
- ☹ Don't give up too early, thinking that the positives aren't making a difference. (One motivational speech does not net a successful CEO.)
- ☺ Repeat the voices of positivity each day. Take action, selfless action in service to others. You get to be a successful CEO through repetition of positives.
- ☹ Don't fall into the trap of thinking there will not be any more risks in your life.
- ☺ Retrain your brain (work it, sister, every day) to be more positive—this creates less time and effort to move through future challenges.

IDEAS FOR PULLING MORE POSITIVE INFLUENCES INTO YOUR LIFE

Definitely do these when risk-taking and challenges are imminent. Double do them when you're in active, swamp-wading mode.

- Spend time with positive family and friends
- Get a dedicated coach, trainer, and/or mentor
- Find a committed accountability partner
- Join a network or group of like-minded people
- Round up motivational and inspirational videos (TED Talks)
- Read books—biographies of successful people, inspirational, motivational

- Listen to music, attend plays and galleries: learn the artists' struggles.
- Seek out the stories of successful sports figures, business people
- Expose your brain to mindful quotes
- Subscribe to articles, pages, and websites which encourage positivity
- Look to mentors and success models: game-changers and influencers such as Tony Robbins and Oprah Winfrey

Smile more: at least twenty times a day. Smile at strangers and co-workers (even if they are frowning). Engage those mirror neurons and influence people around you to be more positive.

Listen Jane, Listen

Hindsight is always twenty-twenty.

I'd made so much progress. A different woman. Jack had noticed too.

I'd made my list of things that I needed in order to feel loved—though I hadn't shared it with him—but my attitude had shifted. I meditated, I ran, hiked, I ate chia jam, the kids ate chia jam, we all ate chia jam.

Sessions with Grace were still filled with learning. Still, my mind drifted to times before the kids.

I remembered how people would tell me before I had kids that parenting was challenging and difficult, but I would think, "It can't be that bad. I'm sure I'll be okay and manage."

I remember thinking, it can't be harder than calculus. And I'd struggled through that and graduated. It was laughable, my before-parenting beliefs, comparing raising children to calculus.

There is no word for the challenge of parenting. It's something we do for the rest of our life, no breaks, no graduation.

In the beginning, it was a constant drain on me to care for the physical well-being of myself, let alone an infant. And I felt guilty about that. Other mothers seemed to have it down pat.

Sleep-deprived from waking up during the night to feed a baby, stressing about new rashes, wondering why I couldn't breast feed like everyone else, and later constantly worrying about what the baby might put into his mouth; hovering so he didn't fall down the stairs or run into the street. And then another child came along. One became two.

And then it changed as they got older. But that change wasn't easier. Only different. Instead of worrying about protecting them from physical danger, it transitioned, and I started to worry about emotional danger. I'd think, "don't let them feel or hurt like I did emotionally." Deep down, the real reason to protect them from emotional danger, which I've never expressed out loud, was to prevent me from being forced to relive my own terrible emotional experiences.

And of course it continued; nagging them to brush their teeth, take a shower, do their homework, read their books, get their equipment ready for hockey and dance, ask if they signed the birthday card—whose birthday party is it this time? Did I ask one of them to take out the garbage?

My life, like that of many parents, began to meld into theirs, and I felt like I suddenly woke up one day questioning whose life was whose, and started to wonder what had happened to my life. My own life. The life where I did what I wanted, when I wanted. The problem was that I didn't even know what I wanted anymore. Do I stay married? Do I get a job? Do I find a hobby? Do I get out of bed?

My children's personalities were blooming.

And I was happy about that. And I was miserable about how much energy that sucked out of mine.

Our children are never carbon copies of us. My son differed from me quite a bit. I felt like I couldn't connect with him like I used to because he wasn't my baby anymore. He was his own person. The problem was that mama bear was constantly jumping in trying to save him from any possible emotional danger. It was a constant stress. An impossible feat to win. And each day I felt like we were growing apart.

Then one day I'd stopped myself in my thoughts. "Stop being negative, Jane, and find some positive influences," I told myself.

I'd dragged my butt across the room, turned on my phone, and found a ten-minute positivity video that Grace had on her website. I felt an ounce better. A whole ounce.

Then I opened my binder from my coaching sessions and read the material from our latest meeting. We'd talked about metaprograms. Not that I'd heard of them before.

I reflected for a moment, pulled out a piece of paper, and began to list my son's characteristics. I identified that my son is a move away from thinker, he's in it for self, sees the differences, is kinesthetic and processes information over a period of time—not just once, he does things out of necessity and likes to be alone. Then I repeated the process and listed mine.

Holy shit. I realized that my son wasn't the problem at all. I was. I was communicating with him all wrong and setting unrealistic expectations.

I cheered my discovery.

No wonder we weren't connecting. I was completely opposite in each one of those categories.

What a relief. I wanted to scream it out of the window: "I'm not a bad parent after all. I just didn't understand our communication styles. I wasn't respecting the way he processed information and as a result he was frustrated, feeling disappointed with himself, and pushing away from me. I totally get it." I sent an email to Grace instead.

Kids look up to their parents. Parents are the two people they seek approval and validation from the most. I knew I needed to remain conscious of this. I needed to ensure always to respect his authentic self as he grows and learns, and allow him to let his true self shine alongside me. Not the same as me.

That morning at home, with my chia jam on gluten free, I realized the journey wasn't only about me learning how to love myself. It's also about learning how to love my kids so they can love themselves. I didn't need to force my son to change paths; I need to be there to support him as he walks down his. I was also trying to save him from 'my' own emotional dangers. Not his.

I was shocked by my revelations. I thought about sending another note to Grace to tell her I did the work on my own without running to food. That I'd looked for positive influences and dealt with the issue that was bothering me. It felt phenomenal. What a strange new feeling. Instead, I wrote in my gratitude journal, then I looked out the window.

It was cold, and there was a weird storm front happening—the kind that made early June feel like November. I grabbed my sneakers and padded down to the basement. Then, with a smile on my face, I climbed on the treadmill and pressed start. This afternoon, I told myself, I'm buying an insulated jacket.

The next day I saw Grace in her office. She showed me a piece from Ed Sheeran.

> I was a very, very weird child… If you end up being the cool kid in class you'll end up being very boring. Be yourself. Embrace your quirks. Being weird is a wonderful thing. I did alright. You can do alright as well.

I wanted to say that was easy for Ed to say, and even easy for her to believe it was okay to say that. She had an office, framed certificates on the wall. Then I remembered she had kids, and she had stayed home for a while too.

Ed's success and Grace's certificates took me to a dark place. An upcoming function with Jack's company.

I knew people would ask me what I did. I was ashamed to say 'stay at home with the kids'. I had no excuse to not work. It's not like I had a disability that prevented me. It reminded me of my financial dependence on my husband. I cringed. He worked hard. I was an expense.

I felt like when I told people I was a stay-home mom that they didn't see me as an equal. Like I was a lesser.

It made me regret that I sacrificed my career to be a stay-home mom. I felt almost resentful. I thought it seemed like a good idea to be home with the kids. I didn't think finding a job, later, would be so difficult because I assumed I would just pick up where I left off, like riding a bike.

In the last six months, I'd lost count of how many resumes I'd sent out; the number of callbacks was easy to remember. Zero. What a complete failure.

"Nobody wants me. I am not an equal." I poured all that and more out to Grace.

She chimed in. "Jane, it's about how we carry ourselves and the inner confidence we evoke. It doesn't even matter what everyone else's opinion is of you. What matters is whether you see yourself as an equal, and what gifts and value you bring to the world. Jane, if you sit tall, speak with conviction, and talk about something you're really passionate about, people will be so attracted to you. If you tell them that you are pursuing a dream and taking the time to find your dream job, they will not look down on you, but look at you in awe and inspiration."

My spine straightened.

"You have it backwards. You are doing what many people can't do… you are pursuing your passion. That is scary and difficult and takes courage. To me, that sounds like you are as equal as everyone else. Just because other people have found their career or passion, but you haven't, doesn't mean you're not equal. You are."

Another tissue appeared in the blur ahead of me.

"You are on your path to creating that career you dream about. You have to believe you are an equal and then claim respect from other people as an equal. And trust me, if someone legitimately didn't see you as an equal, but you believed that you were, you would have walked out within minutes, knowing you deserved to be treated better. Be a friendly companion to yourself, Jane. You deserve that."

Eyes had to be red, but I knew she looked at me supportively.

She was right. I was blaming everyone else for not seeing me as an equal when all this time it was me. Sometimes hearing the truth hurts. "I actually said they made me feel..." I said.

Here I was, teetering on forty years old, still figuring out what I wanted to do with my life when I grew up. Yet somehow talking to Grace about it made me feel okay with it. I was actively raising wonderful kids. I took care of everything around the house so my Jack didn't have to. I did my share. I was also taking the time to figure out my passion.

Grace had made some suggestions in a previous session and I was out exploring new things. I had drilled down on a few. I knew I had a desire to help people. I knew I loved wellness. I'd enrolled in a few cooking classes and signed up for a nutrition course. I just had to be patient with the process. As long as I was committed, I knew I would figure it out. I knew I would find the right job, even if I had to start over. I was looking at my life as one big disappointment when opportunities were floating all around me. I just didn't look up.

"Jane, I want to ask you a couple of questions since today we are talking about self-limiting beliefs."

"Just let me blow my nose," I said. Then I honked away and I laughed out loud. "Oh God, Grace. Personal growth can be a bitch."

She spat out some of the water she was drinking. I tossed her the tissue box.

"As a child, whose love did you crave the most?" Grace asked.

Stunned was I; never been asked that before. Wasn't sure I could answer it.

"Well, okay." I took a few swigs of water, closed my eyes, and let my mind answer it uncensored. "I'd have to say it was my dad's. When I was a kid, my dad was busy, and he was intimidating; not the most welcoming or affectionate person. He was busy farming, coaching baseball, volunteering on boards. He spent a lot of time with my brothers. Seemed he went to a lot of functions too. Not much time for me. Certainly no one-on-one."

"Why did you crave his love?"

"I'm not sure. I guess because I looked up to him and wanted to make him proud."

"How did you feel you had to be as a result, and what behavior did you develop due to this?"

Places I had never wandered to for what seemed an eternity, places that I stuffed down with chocolate and chips, were surfacing. I got a little itchy.

"He was busy, and I wanted to stay out of the way, so I felt I had to accept that my needs came last. I began believing there were more important issues that needed to be addressed before mine. I started to believe, I guess, subconsciously, that I wasn't important. That it was okay to put my needs last."

This time she handed me the box of tissues. Thank goodness it was super-sized.

"Gosh, I hold no anger or regret or negative feeling towards my dad because he wasn't aware of how I needed to feel loved. I never spoke up. I never asked. I understand he had struggles too, and that he wasn't aware of how his actions impacted me. Through this I found my independence, my ambition, my motivation and my take charge initiative. Without it, I wouldn't be the person I am today. I wouldn't change a thing. I love these qualities about myself, and if that is how I had to get them, then I guess I accept that. It also makes me aware that I can't just wait for someone to guess what I need. Sometimes I have to have the courage to speak up and ask for help or ask for what I need. I deserve it."

"He provided us a good home. I had everything I needed. I just felt excluded and unrecognized by him. I guess I just learned to put my needs last, and rely on myself, so I wasn't an inconvenience to anyone. I didn't like to ask for help or be a bother to anyone. I never realized this at the time but, reflecting on it now, this belief played into my relationships later on. In every relationship later on in life, I remember asking myself, 'how could this person always put work or friends or life before me?' when I thought that it made me feel unloved. I just let them do it though. I accepted it, accommodated the other person… Ah, it was a pattern; I believed my needs came last, huh?"

I began to talk about an experience that stood out in my mind. I was sitting in the doctor's office with my son who was two. He had a flu bug, and was so sick, the poor guy. We were there for hours, and I hadn't packed enough snacks because I hadn't expected to be there that long. My son was getting really restless and my patience was wearing so thin. I called Jack to give him an update. He said he would come and help me out, but I didn't want him to take time off work just to sit at the doctor's office with me. I could handle it on my own. I was capable. The thing is, Jack showed up half an hour later with some snacks for our son and for me. I was so happy to see him and felt so special he would do that for me. But at the same time I felt so guilty. I told him he didn't have to do that. He didn't have to take time off work. He simply replied, "I know I didn't have to, but I wanted to and I chose to." That hit me deep. He wanted to go out of his way for me. It made me feel so special.

I said it out loud without thinking: "Where has that husband gone? Where has the husband who used to be there for me gone? I feel like that relationship we once had is completely lost to now being roommates who pay bills and chauffeur kids back and forth to their activities."

"Jane, how did or can this experience make you a stronger and better person? What can you learn from it?" asked Grace.

My chest opened. Had the weight on it been so heavy? I breathed in and out, deeper than in meditation. I felt as if I'd let go of a heavy burden.

I'd thought keeping this stuff in was better than talking about it because I thought there wasn't anything I could do to change the past. But it wasn't about changing the past. It was about letting it go and allowing myself to move on with new beliefs that serve me in my today world, identifying who I am and who I want to be.

I realized that, in order for me to feel loved and significant, I needed to put my needs first; even ten minutes in the shower had shown me that.

Asking for what I want takes some strength from me. I'm not used to it. I am used to people just telling me.

I sat in the quiet of Grace's office, a super-comfortable silence, and thought to myself: people cannot read minds so I don't need to make them guess. I don't get mad or assume things because I think they should just know. If I tell others what I need; it gives them a better chance to successfully provide it.

"Expecting others to guess what we need is not a condition of how we need to be loved. It makes it very limiting. Am I the last person on the planet to find this stuff out?" I asked.

I handed back the box of tissues. "If I look at my marriage, I haven't done that; I've put myself last. I haven't voiced what I need. I've expected Jack to know what I need."

"So, Jane, talk about your husband. Just briefly. What do you need in order to feel loved by him?"

Holy crap, that slapped me across the face. I had no idea. If I had no idea, how on earth could he?

When I told Grace I had no idea, she said that was okay. She gave me some homework. To think and explore ideas of what 'I' needed to feel loved by Jack. She explained that, once I knew what I needed, I could enlighten him, and if he chose to ignore those needs, we'd cross that bridge then. "For now, I just want you to think about what you need."

"Okay, I can do that."

"Fantastic. So here's a concept," she said. "When we drive a car, we spend most of our time looking through the windshield and only occasionally check the side and rear view mirrors. Yet most of us spend our time moving through life by looking at the rear view and side mirrors. If you or I drove like that, we wouldn't make it down the street. We must learn to retrain our minds to start looking through the windshield. We must focus on our own road instead of being so concerned about everyone else's."

I pictured the massive windscreen in the SUV, and then the smaller mirrors. Did I even have one on the passenger side? I mainly used the windshield when I drove.

"I'm so proud of you today," said Grace. "These were big releases and very tough questions to face and answer. You did so great and are so much more confident and strong and inspiring than you realize."

Then she hugged me. A big comforting, everything is going to be alright, kind of hug.

I thought to myself how funny that I hated this person an hour before when she called me out, but now saw where she was going and was so grateful to have her make me start to see myself and my relationships in a new light.

"My needs are not going to come last any longer", I told myself all the way home. I am not going to feel guilty for it. I also need my husband to make me feel special by spending time with me with the TV off, just talking about life—like when we first started dating.

That night I came up with more things: I want him to take time for me, just the two of us, and not be on his phone or distracted with thoughts about work.

I need him to engage with me and be interested in what I am saying and in what I am doing. I don't need constant physical connection. I need emotional connection.

And another switch turned on. Just like the chia jam, the bread, the running, I saw another need: to give him love in his currency as well as for him to give me love in mine. I wasn't sure how I was going to bring this up or how we would restart after all these years, but at least I had figured out what I wanted and needed. I decided, whether he wants this relationship to work or not, I know what I want, and I can move forward from that instead of feeling so stuck.

For the first time in ages I began to believe I was worthy. Maybe it was for the first time, I decided. Maybe even more than I had when I was younger.

I thought more about Grace's questions:
"Whose love did you crave the most?"
"Why did you crave their love?"
"How did you feel you had 'to be' as a result?"

"What behavior did you develop due to this?"
"How did/can this experience make you a stronger and better person?"

I closed my journal, turned off the living room lamp, peeked in on the kids, and then joined the snorer. When I closed my eyes the concept danced into my dreams: the past does not equal the future. You can change course anytime you choose.

We cannot change the cards we are dealt, just how we play the hand.
                                                    Randy Pausch

PART V
ROMANCING THE SELF: LOVE AND AUTHENTICITY OF COLLATERAL HAPPINESS

Self Love
Six Core Human Needs
Forgiveness and Acceptance of Self

Authenticity
Stepping Outside Our Comfort Zone
Facing Our Fears

*In a perfectly imperfect world,
Sometimes to find balance,
You first have to lose balance.
Own every second,
Every broken heart,
And shout, "I loved. I learned. I grew."*

Step Six:
A Primer On Self Love

When we struggle to find love for our self, it becomes easier to focus on others as a way to hide our own sense of fear and disappointment.

Hiding behind, and confining ourselves to, the concerns and burdens of others is a way to evade our own problems by convincing ourselves we need to fix someone else's.

When we do this, we distract ourselves from admitting what is amiss in our own life.

No matter how much we put it off, at some point we need to face our inner demon and learn to love our self.

Self-Love #1: Six Core Human Needs

There are six core universal needs that drive all human behavior and form the basis of every decision we make, paraphrasing Tony Robbins.

Each individual has these same six needs. However, the priority and meaning of each need, for each individual, is what determines the direction of each person's life. Humans are innately compelled to fulfill these six needs and do so in either constructive or destructive ways. Awareness and understanding of these needs is directly related to our capacity for self-love and fulfillment. If 'unfulfillment' and unhappiness arises, ask yourself which of these needs is unfulfilled and what you need in order to fill it.

Need 1: Certainty/Comfort
Comfort, familiarity, and stability, along with the need to avoid pain, are human nature. Our need for certainty is a survival mechanism, affecting how much risk we're willing to take in life—career, finances, and relationships. The higher our need for certainty, the less risk we are willing to tolerate. Control and predictability makes us feel secure.

Need 2: Adventure/Variety
To feel excitement, undertake adventure, and accept change is natural as well. The best way to describe this need is by asking the question, do you like surprises? If you answered "yes," you're fooling yourself. We only like the surprises we want. The ones we don't desire, we refer to as problems. **Problems are opportunities to help us grow.** They fulfill our need for variety.

Need 3: Significance
This is our need to feel important, special, unique, and/or needed. It's our desire to feel worthy of love and attention, and to stand out from the crowd. The ultimate feeling of significance comes from intrinsic rewards as opposed to external sources. It is fulfilled by establishing our sense of self-esteem and feeling good about our self.

Need 4: Love & Connection
Our oxygen of life; what we all desire and need most. To feel communication, approval, intimacy, and to be loved by others. When we give and receive love completely, we feel alive. When we lose love, the desire still exists, except we find ourselves settling on connection—the fragments of love—in any way we can find.

The next two needs are rarer; not everyone meets these needs. The truest form of fulfillment and happiness occurs when we find a way to meet all six needs.

It is important to note that the needs of certainty and variety, significance and love/connection, growth and contribution, work together in the law of balance. The needs complement each other as a paradox—to push and pull us towards fulfillment. If we have too much of one, it will compromise another. The key to fulfillment and happiness is to recognize how to live in the balance point between the two polarities. It is important to recognize what we require in order to fulfill each need.

Need 5: Growth
To feel emotional, intellectual, and spiritual personal development. Like a plant: the moment we stop growing we start dying. Growth gives us the ability to express our true creative energy and allows us to help others. Growth is the purpose of life. The more we grow and learn, the more we become attuned with our truest self.

Need 6: Contribution

Contribution is a sign of ultimate fulfillment. It is the need to give beyond our self and to help and serve others. Sharing and giving enhances everything we experience. It is important to note that we can only give what we have (not more). If we want to contribute more, we need to find a way to fill our own bucket first. In addition: giving while expecting reciprocity only ends up in resentment. We can only give what we are capable of giving.

Own It Jane, Own It

An anticipated night from hell: the financial year end office party for management. A private room in a restaurant overlooking the 18th hole at the VP's country club. Of course, I wore black.

And, of course, I was asked the question by a manager's new girlfriend, "What do you do?" Thankfully, we were interrupted before I had to answer. I excused myself and sat on the toilet seat lid in a cubicle in the washroom and wondered how I would answer that question, if asked again.

I pondered how many unhappy women had sat in this very cubicle. I thought about office cubicles. I imagined a desk where the inside of the washroom door was, at the height of an advertisement for condoms and safe sex. I hoped that there was the same in the men's washrooms, or at least near the urinal. Safe sex is everybody's responsibility. Sex? When had I last had sex? Was Jack having sex with someone like his co-worker's girlfriend who was half his age?

And then I heard the heels of shoes click by. Black patent, not unlike my own, and a decent set of ankles, not unlike my own. A cubicle door banged and the slide of a lock in place, then shuffling and a woman's voice. "It's me," she said. "Yes, it's dreadful. I'll see you later. Of course I'll get away. It's migraine season."

I didn't recognize the voice as anyone in our party, but I recognized the deceit.

In one fell swoop I decided I didn't want my life to be lived in the toilet.

I left black-shoe-woman to her conversation. Back in the restaurant, the wine flowed freely. The girlfriend was young, but apparently had already passed her bar exams and was employed with a local law firm.

She engaged quickly. "You were going to tell me where you worked," she said.

"I'm glad you asked," I said. "There are a few things under consideration, but one thing is certain, I will be running my own company."

Jack's head swiveled. "I've renewed my passion for running," I said. "I've been involved with a group at The Stable Cafe. I'm seriously considering starting a wellness advocacy. I want to combine wellness with, well, wellness."

"Oh my God, that's so clever," said the girlfriend.

A hand gripped my own under the table. My eyes teared as my fingers remembered the profile of Jack's hand.

Girlfriend asked something else, but I was so lost in Jack's squeeze that I couldn't focus. A good thing, because I later thought that this would have been a time to let my ego calm, to only speak my truth, but not to put down anyone else's goals or achievements.

"I'd love to get your take on the corporate dog eat dog," said the girlfriend. She leaned forward and whispered, "Being a lawyer isn't what I thought it would be. All that money for my education."

"I can recommend a book," I said. She offered her phone for me to type in the title.

"So what's that going to cost you, Jack?" One of the guys had overheard. "Startups are expensive." His wife remained silent by his side.

Jack continued to hold my hand. I thought: come on, say something, Jack. Then I thought, no, I can speak for myself.

"Jack will only gain," I said. And, as I delivered those words, I glimpsed my old self in his wife. I so wanted to check under the table to look at her shoes.

I excused myself again; teetered on the fricking too-high heels, and checked my ego.

Then I vandalized the bathroom. In essence I didn't scratch anything into the door, but I wrote 'There is POWER behind your facade' in lipstick.

I skipped dessert, tolerated the increasing conversational volume, then kissed Jack a passionate goodnight, and said I'd see him later; that I'd received a call about something I had to deal with.

"Who? What?" he asked.

"I'll explain later." I kissed him again.

"I'll come with you," he said.

"No. Celebrate with the guys. Enjoy your year end."

"I won't be long," said Jack.

And I knew he wouldn't, but it didn't matter.

I stepped directly into a taxi and asked to be taken home, but to detour first to the home of a friend—I didn't even know if she still lived there. It had been years. We'd been close, but one day she'd announced she was no longer my friend. It was before I'd had the kids, before I met Jack. I had been thriving at work and enjoying running. She'd said I didn't give her enough attention. She'd said I was too happy.

She was right because I was becoming positive and I didn't enjoy her negative attitude.

All these years I'd thought I wasn't a good friend. I was the bad one, I was rejected; but now I saw that nothing was wrong with either of us. We'd shared a lot. It was time to enter a place that I could see her with love. I didn't want to just move on and forget. I wanted to release all negative emotion that was lingering within myself.

Locked onto a course of forgiveness and acceptance, the taxi turned into the street on which she used to live.

I'd told Grace I would only look through the windshield and not the rear-view mirror. I realized that, to feel free and at peace, I had to release all the negative emotions I still felt toward my friend.

I stepped out of the cab, looked at the house in darkness, and said, "Forgive."

Back at home, I sat outside with a blanket around me and looked at the stars; not as many as I'd remembered from the farm—we were in a city after all.

Forgive. Maybe I'd have it tattooed across my forehead. Well, maybe some other spot.

I was ready to forgive myself for not being who I thought I should be, and accept who I actually was.

Self-Love #2: Forgiveness and Acceptance of Self

The process of forgiving and accepting self helps us identify our positive qualities of identity. Doing this helps us build a stronger sense of worth and esteem. When we value ourselves more, we can begin to let go of the pain that may be holding us back. The less pain we hold, the more space there is for love to enter.

The first step in self-forgiveness and self-acceptance is recognizing that each part of us is wonderful. Letting go of negative self-judgement allows us to learn to enjoy being who we actually are, not who we think we should be. In order to be fully happy, we need to be and own who we really are, and trust what we feel inside—our instincts—rejecting what people, society, culture expects of us.

It is important to stop beating ourselves up for not meeting expectations as planned, or for not being the person we thought we would be. It is great to have high standards and strive to attain large goals. As we move toward our goals we need to view ourselves through loving eyes; it does no good to border on self-abuse in the process of achieving. Berating ourselves about how we haven't succeeded, or haven't become who we thought we should, sinks the spirit. In training our minds to love ourselves unconditionally we become our own best cheerer and friend.

Holding onto vengeance, anger, or shame doesn't affect anyone other than the self. As hard as it might be to admit, the people or situations that have caused pain for us are also those who have made us stronger—better versions of ourselves. We need to learn how to see past negative emotion. It is important to forgive others, just as it is important to forgive ourselves.

In order to really let go of the past and focus positively on the future, first recognize the lessons, then learn to forgive ourselves for any attached negative belief.

Brené Brown, through her work that features the study of vulnerability and shame, explains that one has to heal shame through vulnerability and empathy.

Many of us, despite experiencing empathy, can still feel the pain of old wounds. This triggers shame. The result is that we cannot fully move on and heal when under the influence of shame. In order to move on, we need to understand and use empathy as a critical first step. And, after that first step, we need to truly forgive and accept ourselves in order to fully heal.

STEPS OF SELF-FORGIVENESS FOR INDIVIDUALS

1. Identify all regret, shame, pain, discontent, anger or failure that stands out in your life. Is there any pattern that may present itself?

2. Share your experiences with someone you completely trust. This helps create empathy.

3. Detach from seeing the situation through your current eyes; recognize that, when you made certain decisions, you didn't know then what you know today. You did your best given the information at the time. Your values were different than they are today. You didn't know at the time what the consequences or outcome would be as a result of your actions. You didn't know how much time would be involved. You were not, and are not, a fortune teller.

4. Detach the negative feeling as part of your identity. You are not a bad person just because you may have done something you, society, or a part of society deems as 'bad', or because you have not achieved yet what you set out to do. Experiences are lessons, not life sentences.

Self-Love #2: Forgiveness and Acceptance of Self

5. Recognize the disconnect between who you actually are and who you think you should be. Bring your focus back to who you currently are. Acknowledge it, and allow yourself to know that who you are today is enough. This person is wonderful. You can remind yourself that you are on the path to becoming who you want to be. It's essential to accept the self in the moment. Accepting who you are allows alignment with the authentic self.

6. Find meaning in the experience. Ask yourself the following questions: "How did this experience make me a stronger, more beautiful person? What trait did I learn/acquire that makes me 'me', and would never give up now that I have it? What can I learn from this experience to ensure I do things differently next time, knowing what I know? What positive belief can I take away from this?"

7. Forgive and accept yourself for being perfectly imperfect. You experienced a valuable lesson. Embrace the opportunity to learn from it, and move on. Don't hold yourself prisoner to negative feelings.

Accept that your awareness is the first step. Awareness is a place from which to work to take this new conscious, positive belief and allow it time to pass from the conscious mind to the subconscious. Allow time to acknowledge when old negative subconscious beliefs interrupt your pattern of growth. It takes a bit more than sixty days to begin to believe the new, truthful story of self.

In order to experience an inner peace and love for self, it is essential to forgive yourself for not being the person you thought you would be, and to accept the person you actually are.

This doesn't mean you can't work toward goals; it just means the gaps need to be acknowledged, and to accept you are a work in progress.

It's productive to separate the 'I want to be a success' from 'I am my authentic self working toward achieving success.'

'I want' means I lack and have not yet got. This creates disharmony in the body, and the feeling of discontent. It's why people continuously chase dreams to 'try' fill the void, yet never feel satisfied when they do.

It also means that what has been done in the past does not become an identity. Your past does not become your permanent identity. You get to choose. We all do. Identity is not attached to the past or the future. It is only attached to the present. This is true for you. This is true for everyone.

If we live in the disappointment of not living up to the expectations of our self, or of others, we will never feel satisfied. We will always live chasing the carrot. Admitting our weaknesses and shortcomings is key to growth. Accepting all parts of the self is paramount to maturity.

Since our actions are determined by our thoughts, it is essential that we start controlling our thoughts so they align with our authentic self, not our ideal self.

When we align our thoughts to our ideal self we dishonor our authentic being which then causes disharmony—physically, mentally, emotionally—within the body. When we align our thoughts to our ideal self, we live in discontent. We create a void which, in the body, can feel like depression, anxiety, anguish, or despair. We then seek to fill this void with artificial happiness measures.

When we associate our identity with the negative opinions or false expectations of people/society/culture, we begin to lose the feeling of acceptance of the self. We begin to feel the discontent of not being good enough. It is important to value other people's opinions as check-ins, but those opinions need not be held with more value than our own. When we start to misalign our identity

Self-Love #2: Forgiveness and Acceptance of Self

with ideal self over authentic self, we live a lie. We lie to ourselves about who we really are.

When we are discontented, we seek artificial means to alleviate the pain, or we may even feel the need to make changes—home, job, friends, partner, and country—to attempt to escape this void. We may find ourselves in a state of being where something feels off, yet we are not sure what. All we know, at those times, is the body is telling us there is something out of balance. The energies of the ideal self and authentic self, when misaligned, give the body a message as a call to action.

When we begin to align our identity to our authentic self of the present, we no longer need the acceptance of others; that void goes away and we begin to love and accept ourselves as we currently are. As enough.

When we are unaware of 'acceptance', most of us want to detach, ignore, or stuff down negative feelings and focus on only the good ones. The negative feelings are calls to action. They are not life sentences for punishment. They are signs that we need to shift a belief about our identity. We typically misunderstand this call to action and blame external sources for our disharmony.

When we accept our authentic self as is, we feel content, which leads to caring less about the opinions of others. We no longer seek to continue to do things to prove to ourselves that we are good enough, because we already accept and believe that we are more than good enough.

Without recognizing this, we may carry on relationships that repeatedly fail. Following this, we may question if there is something wrong with us. At the beginning of a relationship, people tend to be who they think the other person wants to see. As a result, one or both people carry on a charade. Once the other person can no longer keep up with the charade, we begin to see the person's authentic self. If the authentic self causes disharmony, we may feel betrayed or guilty.

It's the same on our turf. The other person sees who he or she wants to see in 'you', for example. If you have not presented as authentic, this view will be totally different than who you are. The game will be up, and you and the other person will know it when there is disharmony.

If we live as who we are, not who we think we should be, our relationships will never falter, because we accept our self and the other person from the beginning.

In relationships we tend to subconsciously mimic what we think the other person desires rather than authentically present who we really are. We do this to receive attention, even love. We often violate the authentic self in order to feel connection with others.

Authentic relationships flourish when both partners get to be their true selves and each person is accepted for all the parts of his or her personality. These are the rare, true gems that present us with the privilege of their presence. Relationships comprising authentic partners are uncommon, since most people are uncomfortable walking in their true essence every hour of every day.

Other people find themselves in situations where one partner eventually does find his or her true essence, while the other does not. This leads to difficult conflicts in relationships where each person begins to question if the relationship is worth preserving. Or we may question whether the person was living a lie and betrayed us. Typically, people do not outright lie to hurt us. They just haven't found the courage to live authentically or learned how to respect others who do.

Why do our past failures and rejections feel like 'falling outs', endings, or betrayals? Because we think we did something wrong or someone did something wrong to us.

Know it wasn't personal. These occurrences were a call to action to reconnect with our true essence. Endings mean new beginnings.

Self-Love #2: Forgiveness and Acceptance of Self

The closer we come to being our authentic self, the less we tolerate anything that is inauthentic. The price of authenticity is giving up and releasing all that is inauthentic. It is realignment. Sometimes we create the endings, and other times the universe does it for us. Understanding this makes it easier to forgive and accept.

UP CLOSE AND PERSONAL

As you walk in your 'true' essence, if you discover you're in a relationship that does not align, do not question whether there is something wrong with you; simply accept that your values and those of the other person do not match.

When individuals do not align with an authentic self, there is the tendency to 'control' or over compensate. It's a human subliminal attempt to prevent people or situations from shaking the sense of self.

The only control in the world we have is over our own body, mind and spirit. Everything else is an illusion.

Seeking another person's approval does not equal acceptance of self. We can't accept self until we do the work to determine who it is that we actually are. Until we determine who we are and accept our present self, we will continuously seek to find external approvals to fill in the void.

REPEAT TO YOURSELF AS OFTEN AS YOU NEED

"I choose to like me. I choose to approve of me. I choose to accept me, all aspects of me, even the 'unlikeable' parts. I forgive myself for falling short of expectations and making mistakes. Humans are not perfect, therefore I am not a mistake nor are the people around me. We are students, learning as we go."

We can each begin to stop forcing relationships when we each accept our authentic self of the present.

We 'learn' to love ourselves through the acceptance of self and the positive awareness of our lessons.

We cannot speak 'love for self' into existence. We build our character one piece at a time upon the positive traits, and we learn from the negative experiences, in order to get closer to revealing our authentic self.

Not only is it a challenging lesson to learn to love our self, we are also required to learn the courage, strength, and faith to let go of anything that is inauthentic.

My past failures and rejections are merely the reality of anything inauthentic to me falling out of my life. It is a call to action to reconnect with my true essence.

Acceptance is the practice of accepting the higher purpose of our being.

The word 'practice' is used intentionally, because acceptance does not come naturally, nor is it passive. Life begins to take on a new rhythm as we practice acceptance and stop working so hard to manipulate expectations. We begin to live in the flow, enduring much less struggle and experiencing much more joy.

To further understand acceptance, it's important to grasp that it is part of the release of grief process. This is why acceptance is not something we easily speak into existence. Imagine how many times someone says, "just get over it, move on, accept this, let it go."

Easily said, yet not easily done.

Why?

Because pain occurs when our 'life model' does not equal 'life experience'. When they don't equal, it can seem like loss—similar to grief. It can be the loss of a tangible 'experience', like a loved one, a job, or health. It can be the loss of an intangible 'model', like an ideal, a goal, a dream, an expectation, our ideal self. Either way, it presents as pain.

To overcome pain, we change either the model or the experience. To change, we accept the loss of the old model and/or experience. To accept, we move through the stages of grief.

Suffering happens when we feel powerless to change either the model or the experience and we do nothing. Struggle is inevitable. Suffering is optional. This does not mean it is easy or effortless. It's a choice. It is a mindset. It is up to each of us to restore our internal power—to make our life model equal our life experience and make our thoughts/feelings align with our actions.

The stages of pain including the loss of a life model or life experience.

1. **Pain:** Life model ≠ life experience. We grieve the loss of the old model and/or experience.

2. **Denial:** This is a state where we just aim to survive the pain by going numb. We avoid. We ignore. We tune out the noise and the people. We live with apathy. Life seems to make no sense and we don't understand our existence. We wonder what the point of life or having dreams is, and question whether there is a reason to continue. As we move though denial, we eventually begin to ask ourselves questions which point us in the direction of lifting the veil of numbness.

3. **Anger:** Anger offsets denial. In order to oppose the force of feeling withdrawn and numb, we create anger to help balance the body. Anger hides our true pain. In anger, we tend to shift responsibility, blaming others for our pain and mistakes. We say to ourselves that this occurred because of the kids, spouse, parents, friends, boss, God.

   Blame is a shift of energy from our self to others. We blame others for our mistakes because it temporarily allows us to make sense of the situation. We can take a breather by thinking it is not our responsibility or fault. We blame because we create rules for our model of life that only we are aware of, yet assume everyone else must instinctively know.

Blame may feel good as it offsets the feeling of denial, but, it causes us to give away and relinquish power. When we give away power, we are no longer in control of our life or our model. When we feel powerless, it extends our suffering. When we begin to take responsibility for our pain is when we can move on to the next stage of the healing process.

4. **Bargaining:** This is when we take up our one-on-one with God or some higher power. "Please God make this go away. Please take this pain from me and I will be able better to help others." We wait around for a saving grace to fall in our laps and pull us out of the trenches. We can't bear to think we have to do the work on our own. There must be a God or grace or 'expert' that will just do it for us. We don't want to change. We want to hold on to the last threads of what we currently have. We ponder how we could go back in time to get a redo, or stop that pain from ever happening. We ask ourselves, what if's, if only's, should haves and maybe's. We assess what we could have done differently in the past so as to not experience the pain now. We resist the idea of changing. We remain living in the past, where the pain did not exist, and put off for days, months, years, the reality of the present.

5. **Depression:** When we begin to pull ourselves out of the past and into the present, we enter into depression. This stage feels as though it will last forever. We come to terms with the current reality and feel powerless when our life model does not equal our life reality. We may withdraw from life, and feel a veil of sadness overcome us. We are saddened by the loss of a past goal not coming to reality or fruition. We are depressed that what we thought would happen did not, or who we should have become did not happen either. It can become a coping mechanism, an excuse, distraction, justification to stay the same. Change is resisted. Depression is a step in the

right direction because we have at least moved from living in the past to living in the present. If we keep comparing our present 'self' to an ideal, it will be never be possible to be fully happy and accept who we currently are.

6. **The Crazy 8:** Just because the stages are written in a linear pattern does not mean the stages occur in that same fashion. After minutes or hours of bargaining or anger, we may find ourselves right back at denial and seeking to feel numb again. It is a cycle that can repeat like a Crazy 8 emotional swing. When depressive states like sadness, despair, shame, guilt, loneliness, or anxiety reach a critical level—nothing has happened to resolve the issue—we can shift, sometimes quickly and unexpectedly, to anger, blame, defiance, resentment, frustration, or aggression. Anger states bring a powerful dopamine hit to offset the low of depressive states. The anger energy state stays active for a period of time, but if no resolution comes with it, it subsides, and we fall back into the depressive state; thus the Crazy 8 swing. To deal with this transfer of states, we may distract ourselves with artificial happiness means—food, drugs, gambling, shopping.

7. **Acceptance:** This is the final stage when we let go. We accept the present model and experience including our current authentic self. This occurs when we are ready to give up the artificial happiness means and decide to take the positive path to collateral happiness. We accept our current reality. We get to a place where we look back on the whole situation and see it as a blessing in disguise. It may not have been what we planned or even wanted, but in the end it was what was needed to help us realign to our higher self and to help us get closer to maximizing our full potential. Endings = new beginnings, new opportunities.

8. **Change:** We choose to change our life model and our rules. We begin to work changing our strategy, story and state of mind. We ask ourselves what we really need in order to feel fulfilled and leave behind the pain. We shift our focus from that of our pain being pointless to looking at it as a learning

opportunity. Change does not mean we are completely alright and the situation is dismissed. (Remember, it takes a new conscious thought at least 60 days of repetition to become subconscious.) It will take time to heal and move on from the loss, and we will begin to:

- find a way to live with our new norm;
- find a way to change our life model;
- think of new goals and new dreams;
- reorganize our life and our patterns;
- change our beliefs;
- enter into new, positive influences;
- allow ourselves to enjoy life again—our new life;
- find new meaning and new hope;
- address our weaknesses and seek solutions;
- allow all positives and negatives to surface;
- identify and understand what core needs require addressing.

We change. We grow. We evolve.

Goodbye (old) Jane, Goodbye

✓ Movement.
✓ Food.
✓ Spirituality.
✓ Forgiveness.

I'm not saying it was all a walk in the park. I still found myself in situations. Not everything was worked out.

So, two days after a meeting with Grace, I found myself in a conflict with one of my besties—one of the past girls-nights-outers who had moved out of town the previous year.

One of the other girls, Liz, called me and said Barb was coming into town for her daughter's dance recital. Liz was organizing a get together. The next thing I knew I felt neglected. Barb was staying at Liz's house.

On paper, like in theory, I understood that I do not have to come first in Barb's life. But I struggled with it and thought about asking her why she hadn't let me know and why she wasn't staying with me. I thought we were closer.

Should I confront her or keep it to myself? I knew if I chose the latter I'd feel further disconnection.

I started creating a story in my head as my own past issues of rejection began to surface. I thought, maybe I was not as important to her as I thought. I considered, momentarily and subconsciously, why not reject her before she has the chance to reject me?

I decided to tell her that I was feeling neglected. I went in with an open mind and good intentions, but suddenly, with one small comment from her, blinded by my hurt, I misunderstood the comment, and my good intentions of telling her how I felt turned into a battle of who was right and who was justified.

Grace had given me the opportunity to practice what I'd learned, and I'd blown it. I thought that, sometimes, books or counselling sessions do not take into account that we cannot instantly turn ourselves on or off, with a flick of a switch, just because we say we can. In times of emotion, we can look at our outer selves and see the crazy, yet can't find the switch to turn it off. We can only feel the emotion.

Here I was trying to feel closer to my bestie, and instead I was saying all the wrong things and causing us both to feel hurt.

I reflected and wanted to figure out how I needed to move from feeling hurt to feeling happy so I could tell my bestie what was really going on inside my head; feel connected rather than disconnected.

My first approach was to do what every person suggests: I waited a few hours to settle the emotion.

With time on my side, I broached the subject with her, yet with one small comment the emotion came right back to surface. Even though I was trying to be good about it, I was saying things that made both of us feel worse. But, the problem was, I was now committed to the conversation, and I couldn't just walk away in mid-disagreement. It was left unresolved.

I slept on it and in the morning it became clear to me.

In order to move on, I had to learn to communicate with myself first before I applied the skills of communication between two people.

I channeled my 'inner Grace' by reflecting on what it was that I really wanted and on what was hurting me. I asked myself what basic need of mine felt violated or hurt. I recognized it was this:

my need for love and connection. I realized that my hurt stemmed from my need to feel reminded that she thought I was still just as important to her as she was to me.

I did an inner-Jane-TED-talk and started it with the realization that in a marriage or a friendship it is assumed that we love each other. But in order for a marriage or friendship to flourish and stay happy, we cannot assume it. It's so important to remind our loved ones how much they mean to us—through words or through action.

I finally understood that I needed to start the conversation with her as this, "I recognize that you and I are busy with work, and kids, and daily chores, but I am asking for a reminder that I am important to you because you are important to me."

Saying this initially, would have saved the quarrelling of who was right. We would have stopped talking about the surface things and started talking about what was real.

I did not care if she stayed at Liz's. I just needed a reminder that I too was important.

After I recognized this, the weight on me lifted. I needed to communicate to her why I was feeling hurt. I also needed to invite her to tell me what she needed from me.

I realized that as much as we all might hate conflict, sometimes it's that conflict that is needed in order to bring us closer to the people that we love.

I also learned that sometimes I need to sit down with the people I love and learn what it is they need from me. Sometimes I need to do things I do not enjoy, not for my sake, but for theirs, because it is important to them.

Since certain people are important to me, I need to do things for them in order to honour our connection. It's not all about me. I am not the centre of the universe. To have connection, I choose to be willing to use different love currencies—mine and the other person's. The exchange that takes place deepens our connection.

Because Barb did not come to visit me, she hurt me. Because I said I did not want to attend the dance recital, I hurt Barb. We both loved each other. Somewhere along our friendship, we just began exchanging the wrong love currencies with each other. The goal is not to be right; it is to provide love in the other person's love currency in order to increase connection.

The biggest lesson was to become aware of the root of my pain. To communicate with myself before I communicate with others.

Sometimes, when we hurt the ones we love, it is usually without intention and awareness. Conflict can be dissolved if we first communicate with ourselves what it is we need and then speak to others with this in mind. Knowing how we ourselves hurt, and knowing what we want, prevents us from arguing, blaming, and insulting others.

I drove over and apologized. I owned my misperception. We hugged.

I swear there were mornings I didn't recognize myself in the mirror. Sometimes I was totally clueless, and other times my smile was ear to ear confidence.

Step Seven:
Revealing Our Authentic Self

The authentic self can be called the 'third' brain—our essence and true identity. The authentic self is often masked by the facade of our ego and cognitive brain.

But make no mistake; our silent inner-knowing of authentic self never leaves us alone. It is always there, even if a faint whisper.

In today's busy world, we become distracted—almost negligent of our true self—and have a tendency to ignore our 'third' brain. We often avoid it or tune it out because there are seemingly more 'pressing' or 'urgent' issues that arise—money, control, reputation, popularity, sensory pleasure, and convenience.

How can we recognize the difference between authentic self and the ego of the cognitive brain? The authentic self can only live in the present moment, not in the future or the past. It is a deep feeling and knowing—a trust of our intuition. The intention in life is to allow the ebb and flow between the authentic self and the ego of the cognitive brain to live within the law of balance. Together they work to help us grow, evolve, and create collateral happiness. Somewhere along our path, we lose touch with this balance and ego's voice becomes the only voice of reason and identity. The result is a deep feeling of emptiness, anxiety, disharmony, depressive tendency—an existential vacuum.

It is only in the quiet contemplation of our stillness that we experience a call, from deep within, to fill the emptiness and express our true selves. Authentic self begs us to set aside the ego in order to be heard.

Part of our adult existence is to unmask, or strip away the facade, we have built over the years—we are meant to reconnect with the authentic self to express our true identity, and to experience true growth. This requires stepping into the zones of discomfort, putting ourselves out there, risking conflict, disappointment, rejection, and failure. In essence, it requires finding the courage to face our fears.

The reward of unmasking is that, once we embrace the opportunity to engage with our third brain, our potential to live to the fullest increases exponentially, and we can experience abundance unlimited.

Authenticity #1:
Stepping Outside Our Comfort Zone

When we consistently distort and silence the authentic self, we begin to lose the desire for life. Without meaning and guidance from this self, a void ensues which we typically seek to fill with artificial means. Choosing comfort at the expense of growth moves us farther from being in touch with the authentic self. It creates listlessness and apathy.

The moment we stop resisting our innate nature of being comfortable and start taking risks to grow our boundaries, our level of discomfort will grow... and so will we.

It's a big feat for each of us to step outside our comfort zone. There's not enough sugar in the world to coat that fact. It takes the kind of work we say we don't have the time, courage, or energy for.

It takes grit to take a public speaking course, quit a dead-end job, initiate a separation and follow through on a divorce.

And yet, how much time, money, and energy have each of us invested in finding 'happiness' the quick and easy way, so that we don't have to deal with the above.

How long have some of us put off a dream, or wondered how to discover a passion? How much time has been wasted and sacrificed? How many relationships have we destroyed, or dishonored, all in the name of remaining comfortable—all so we could avoid change?

Yes, that fretful word 'change'.

We expect everyone or everything around us to change before we consider that we are the ones who need to change; we criticize and judge others because it's our attempt to think they need to change, we need to stay comfortable. We even consider violating our own values just to avoid discomfort. That's how much we as humans are designed to hate discomfort. All in nature's effort to keep us safe.

Be patient, one small step at a time; there is a method to this production. Are you willing to waste any more time? What story are you telling yourself that keeps you from changing?

The first part of stepping out of one's comfort zone is to get comfortable being uncomfortable. What a paradox. Get comfortable with being uncomfortable: a concept echoed many times over, but, for many, never fully embraced.

Thomas Jefferson said it best, "If you want something you've never had you must be willing to do something you've never done."

If we ultimately want to fulfill our need to grow, we will be required to step outside our boundaries of comfort and safety. We will need to do something we have never done.

WHAT DOES IT FEEL LIKE?

It's one thing to acknowledge our comfort zone limits, but another to completely experience stepping out of them.

When we are outside our comfort zone, the face starts to flush; heart beats are rapid; butterflies flutter in the stomach; the body signals 'bathroom time'. There may be nervous ticks or gestures. Hands can flail. Nervous laughter sometimes erupts. We can find ourselves mumbling. Sometimes we avoid eye contact. There's often a lump in the throat. These are all physical symptoms of stepping outside the comfort zone. And always, there are questions including: "Am I making a mistake?" "Is everyone judging me negatively?"

Doubting abilities and waning confidence is a given. Comparisons to others is common. Wallowing in negative self-judgement is a major feature. Excuses arrive in abundance, and confrontation with others can arise just so we can avoid continuing. Sound familiar?

This is what living outside your comfort zone can feel like.

This is the 'condition' (a unique grouping of feelings individual to you) that it's important to get comfortable with.

Comfort zone barriers are what we need to run into and not away from. These are the feelings to become aware of, attune to, and mentally surpass. For some, it gets easier and they are able to do it on their own. For others, the discomfort feels too unbearable, and they require help from others to 'comfort' them. And, fortunately enough, there are many people who want to help. We just need to ask.

The body will always send signals to avoid discomfort; it's the natural reaction of humans. The key is for us to learn how to recognize and override when the body signals us to avoid a change when the purpose is for growth.

We cannot feel bad for feeling these feelings. We all have them. They are all a natural part of the human experience. The only difference is that some people learn how to recognize and embrace it, while others become paralyzed by the experience of growth and stepping outside comfort zones.

One of the things that most people avoid (due to comfort zone limits) is making commitments. Our natural instinct, as humans, is to become procrastinators when our commitments get hard; especially when there's no pressure to complete a task. We easily place our tasks and plans on the back-burner. We justify that

Collateral Happiness: The Power Behind the Facade

there is no need to make a change. We do this just so we can stay comfortable one extra minute, hour, or day.

Note: if you feel this, your employees, kids, spouse, parents feel it too.

Moving through comfort zones in order to grow, and doing so, means feeling uncomfortable.

So, here's a question: when was the last time you felt uncomfortable? Be honest.

Has it been a while?

Take note: The answer to the last time you felt uncomfortable was THE LAST TIME YOU EXPERIENCED GROWTH.

Did you lean into it or run from it?

Conquering discomfort and growth creates natural happy hormones.

Have you become used to feeling comfortable?

If so, the expense of that comfort means you have not been growing. Staying in a place of safety and comfort means you are ignoring the voice of authentic self.

It's the discomfort that we learn to embrace and spend the majority of our life in, not the comfort.

Of course, we can take breaks and breathers, but the goal is to keep growing through the discomfort.

Most people strive to hold onto the 'bliss' moments as long as possible. Most people feel miserable when the 'bliss' moments end quickly. When 'artificial' bliss ends (though we may not have recognized it is or was artificial) we begin questioning our own identity and worth. We often wonder if we've done something wrong. We even question life and the universe itself, and contemplate why 'it' would do this to us.

Nothing is wrong. There is only cause and effect. The negative experiences are a call to action. An invitation to grow. A summon to move toward inner-happiness. A route toward alignment with our true essence.

Discomfort is a course of learning and growth. It develops success, reward, and fulfillment.

When we begin to recognize feelings such as failure and rejection it means we are living our best life. We are experiencing growth. In order to feel authentic inner-happiness we are each required to participate in our own life.

It's difficult to fully appreciate the happy moments in life without juxtaposing them with discomfort. The answer is: stop wasting time and start embracing the comfort zone limits.

Comfort zones are like boxes. It is the placement of those boxes that determines the growth potential.

Imagine standing inside a box that comes up to your ankles. Imagine this box, with you in it, placed on the floor in your living room. When you step over the edge of the box and out into the known area of your living room you may have stepped outside a box but you are still inside the safety of your house. This is not expanding into the growth discomfort zone.

Embracing a 'potential for serious growth' comfort zone is like standing in an ankle deep box, but on the edge of a cliff. The only thing behind you is the jungle from which you came (to which you don't want to return). Above you are clouds and fog, and the limited visibility stretches beyond you. Below is an abyss: black, dark, perhaps bottomless.

Your aim is to leap beyond the clouds, but you have no idea what direction or distance to jump. Memories of past falls evoke fear.

The pulse races. (That's how you know you are in the place—that threshold of growth). Hesitation leaves you standing on the edge, fearful of making the wrong decision. So you do nothing but stand there. You may even begin to make that ankle deep box your home, because you stay so long. Eventually, the thought of leaving the wonderful house you've become attached to is so strong you remain, forever, on the edge, in the box.

You stagnate and wither in discontent and unhappiness.

SO, HOW DO WE ACTUALLY TAKE THE LEAP?

When danger heads our way, the kind that will cause great harm or even death, we jump. It is the only alternative. We rely on desperation. This shock-induced jump can absolutely create growth, but in most cases we wish we would have previously made the choice without having had that kind of push; better it came from a place of sane decision making.

PRACTICAL PRACTICE

Here are six ways to intelligently make the leap beyond the comfort zone.

1. **Knowledge:** using a network of resources—books, videos, and articles—to learn from and then gauge the jump.

2. **Encouragement:** engaging in a supportive team of positive people who will talk us into, not out of, taking the jump.

3. **Faith:** tapping into inspiration to make it a true leap of faith. Having a belief system that there is a 'net' in the abyss that will catch us from falling to the bottom signals that ultimately we believe in ourselves.

4. **Practice:** practice, practice, practice before taking the leap.

The more times we do something, through repetition or role play, the better we get, and the more confident we feel. The more confident we feel, the less risk we sense, and that increases the likelihood that we will leap. When we combine patience with practice, we can anticipate the rewards, celebrate the journey, and confidently accept wherever we land.

5. **Small Steps:** building a bridge. If we take small steps rather than one giant leap, we essentially build a bridge between where we are and where we want to be. There is less risk in small steps. Our brains can handle the risk of small steps. Small-stepped journeys help us appreciate that journey, allowing us to restate and adjust our trajectory.

6. **Mindset:** stopping the chatter of the mind that talks us out of taking the leap. We are hardwired to doubt and second guess. Listening to the self talking us out of a decision to grow is a sad state of affairs, but it is common. Living in a weak, fear based state of mind prevents us from making good decisions. When we focus on the reward rather than the risks (which the chatter of the mind often repeats), and find our inner drive and confidence deep within, we soar. A peak state of mind is achieved by changing our physiology (summoning a smile), altering our language (saying, "I've got this."), and focusing (visualizing the reward).

There is one of two decisions to make when deciding whether to step outside your comfort zone. You either take the risk to jump and embrace the fear, or you stay and embrace stagnation. No right or wrong… only cause and effect.

As difficult as it may be to accept, struggles associated with change are our opportunities for growth. Shifting perspective from focusing on the disappointment of not achieving expectations to enjoying the learning process is a phenomenal achievement in itself. The more we learn the more value we create as a result of our increased proficiency. There is much more satisfaction in living with that perspective. Happy people recognize their lessons rather than dwelling on the failures. They eventually desire more and more lessons and look forward to them.

Focusing on the lack of success in life is unproductive. Seeing all 'things' and 'events' as blessings in disguise advances the growth agenda.

When we focus on lack of success, we diminish the value we have already created. We devalue our authentic Self.

In life it is important to focus on being a really successful student rather than a failed teacher. We have to be the student before we can become the teacher.

If we have a strong sense of self, and an identity built on a strong foundation, we will stop getting stuck each time we find our self at the edge of a comfort zone cliff. Embrace discomfort. Take the leap of growth.

> *People know your name, not your story.*
> *They've heard what you've done,*
> *but not what you've been through.*
> *So take their opinions of you with a grain of salt.*
> *In the end, it's not what others think.*
> *It's what you think about yourself that counts.*
>
> ~ Unknown

If you want to stop being judged by other people, you must first stop judging yourself. EMBRACE all your qualities and SET the course for growth.

At the end of the day, what counts are YOUR true feelings of the joy of being yourself. You need not worry about the judgement of others. To do so is to lose a part of the essence of your true self and to come out of alignment with inner-happiness.

When you take the leap outside your comfort zone, you will leave the comfort of many behind; you will also discover many new friends.

This is true for all of us.

And, for this, we each require a lot of strength and courage to grow.

What's it like on the other side of the comfort zone? After the leap?

Once you take the leap, know it may not be all sunshine and rainbows on the other side. There may or may not be an associated rush of pleasure.

In fact it will most likely still feel uncomfortable. As you find your footing in this new place you may find yourself questioning:

- Was it good enough?
- Can I maintain it?
- Will people accept me?
- Did I get it right?
- Could I have done better?
- Should I go back?
- Why did it take so long?
- Could I have done more?
- Was it worth it?
- Did I look bad?
- Should I quit?
- Is there an easier path?
- Why did it go so badly?

You may even express that you feel dumb, silly, stupid, embarrassed. DON'T go there. Instead, recognize you have found the courage to jump. Incredible courage. The hero of your story. Focus on all the positives.

- Interrupt negative thought patterns.
- Focus on controlling your mindset.
- What are you saying to yourself?
- Rely on your positive influences.
- Let the new settle in.

If we start training ourselves to ask questions like 'what can I learn from this?' or 'what is the opportunity?' and stop asking ourselves 'why did this happen to me?' or 'what is wrong with me?' we can begin to move forward from discomfort.

Authenticity #2: Facing Our Fears

To align with our authentic self, we have to allow ourselves to be vulnerable, and yet possess the courage to face our demons of fear. Each time we face a fear, our boundary grows and with it our sense of self. The larger our sense of self, the more fulfilled we become.

Facing a fear is easier said than done. It is more desirable to accommodate a fear than to face it. Our innate tendency is to control, avoid, reject or insult before we allow ourselves to submit to the vulnerability of facing a fear. Fear based living disconnects us from our true essence. It makes us feel out of control, lose our center of attention, fly off the handle, daydream, lie, cheat or easily get swept off our feet. It 'un-grounds' us spiritually.

Why?

Because fear ultimately threatens our survival.

As stated in the beginning of the book, our bodies are designed for survival. It is the foundation of our existence.

When survival is threatened (perceived through physical or mental stimuli) our right to exist is jeopardized. The systems that kick in when we are under threat may lead us to question or doubt our worth and hinder the ability to attain what we need to thrive.

Feeling like we don't have a right to exist creates a huge void in our being, and causes us to feel like we aren't deserving of life. As a result of this void, we end up settling for less, and begin to create a false sense of security and identity. We lose touch with our true self, which leads to unhappiness and discontent.

We may fool the people around us, but we cannot fool ourselves. Our fear can also jeopardize our other human rights—those natural and moral birthrights possessed by every human being.

- If fear threatens our pleasure and creativity it jeopardizes our right to feel.
- If fear threatens our power and identity it jeopardizes our right to act freely.
- If fear threatens our love it jeopardizes our right to love and feel loved.
- If fear threatens our communication it jeopardizes our right to speak and hear truth.
- If fear threatens our intuition it jeopardizes our right to see/perceive.
- If fear threatens our consciousness it jeopardizes our right to know/have knowledge and understanding.

Loss of these rights leads to a deprivation in health and well-being of our physical, mental, emotional and spiritual self. It causes us to live a disconnected and imbalanced existence, resonating as feelings such as depression, anxiety, anguish, despair. This is why, when we are threatened by the fear of losing any of these rights, it is our instinct to guard them.

We may even do things that bring our character into question; the loss of any of these rights creates a void deep within our being.

With this void present it is impossible to live a life of contentment, so it becomes our choice to fill the void with either authentic or artificial means.

If we want to remove our dependency on artificial means and align our lives closer to our authentic self, the payment required is to address the fear that created the void.

Authenticity #2: Facing Our Fears

That's the most difficult part of the attainment of inner-happiness —addressing the fear that created the void.

Eliminating fears from our life is not the task at hand; the task is learning how to address fears when they arise. The human mind is always going to look for fear because of its instinctual need for survival. There is nothing wrong with us if we are afraid. It is human to be afraid. It is our instinct to guard our birthrights and core human needs. The lesson is to triumph in awareness; to get to know the guards—their shifts, their patterns, and, to the best of our ability, to understand the process of how our guards operate and what keeps them vigilant.

Courage is not the absence of fear, but the ability to endure despite it.

Facing a fear, as difficult as it is, is the most liberating feat we can do for our soul. It reconnects us to our authentic selves, eliminates the threat of losing our rights, and allows us to live in our natural, moral state of being.

Living in fear can feel like a bird trapped inside a cage with the door wide open. The bounds of the cage can feel safe and secure, yet at the same time stagnate growth. The only one keeping you in the cage is you. Do you settle and stay for comfort or escape and leave for growth?

Are you a bird trapped inside a cage with the door wide open? Are you bound by your own fears and expectations that no one is holding you to, except you? If you made the decision to fly, where would you go?

PRACTICAL PRACTICE

So how do we tackle facing a fear?

Train ourselves to start focusing on the reward rather than the penalty.

Focusing on the risk and the penalty keeps us in a fear state of mind. We need to stop dancing around fears, acknowledge them, and then break the fear state by asking a new question: What is the worst that could happen? We are stronger than we give ourselves credit for. The thought, "it might not work out", can be combatted with "it might". We can also ask ourselves, what will we have to sacrifice if we don't deal with this fear?

We can also begin to train the mind to let fear propel and motivate rather than paralyze us. What does this mean? Learn to hate fear. Do not tolerate it. Make fear an unacceptable function of your character. Live for the natural release of happy hormones one feels after facing a fear.

**KEEP ASKING THE QUESTION:
What is the worst that can happen?**

We cannot allow comparisons to, and opinions of, others who build into our fears. We can learn from others who are models of success—mentors—but the only person we can compare ourselves to is 'our own self'. We are not here to impress others. We are here to be our authentic selves.

STOP COMPARING ONESELF TO OTHERS

It helps to address fear by educating our self on what it is we are actually afraid of. Being afraid means we are uncertain. If we take the time to learn and understand what it is we are afraid of, it usually lessens the power of fear. Being uncertain may also create a relentless need for control. When we address fear, we can recognize and let go of all that is not within our control; the only control we have is of our self.

IDENTIFY WHAT CAUSES THE FEAR

The moment we overcome that fear-demon that has been holding us back, we can realize the amazing power we hold in our hands.

Authenticity #2: Facing Our Fears

And it is an amazing life-achievement to understand when we have earned that feeling of conquering fear, for our efforts are truly heroic.

Over time, with experience, we become aware that we don't just survive fears, we actually excel and become better, stronger, and more confident at facing new fears. Each experience is a 'bring it on' moment and then a challenge to grow more.

Raw Jane, Raw

I ran a few 5ks in a couple of months. Sure, I still had fears, but self-confidence was high.

I soon discovered how quickly confidence can wane and fear and shame can step in. They never go away. I learned the mindset to control it.

Jack and the kids and I went on a holiday to Disneyland. We ate, we ate, we ate some more, we lazed by the pool, we toured Universal Studios. We did all the things that tourists do. And we ate some more. When I got back and went to post our photos on Facebook I realized that I'd gained a lot of weight. More than a few pounds. I hadn't thought it possible to do so in such a short time. We'd been back two weeks and my eating habits had not really changed from vacay-mode. It wasn't about the weight, it was about how I felt, right? Did I really believe that? I'd come so far and yet was I still stuck on superficiality?

I didn't want to regress. I wanted to be perfect. My marriage was looking up, I was an active member of the running group, and I was signed up for a psychology course. How could I show myself at the next runner's meeting? How could I go to that course knowing I was a screw up and had just undone all my hard work of becoming healthy?

I had always been competitive growing up. I hadn't realized how much until I'd sort of faded into mom-dom and wife-dom and career-less-ness, and then regained that confidence. With that confidence came that competitive edge. And a powerful ego. All or nothing. I was either perfect or not. What a sham. But, until I dealt with it I knew that I could not, ethically, go out and face others honestly.

I was absolutely terrified to post the pictures. Those photos showing my weight gain were reminders of years of yo-yo dieting.

Posting the pictures would bring judgement—but from whom? *Oh, Jane, you're just like you were before, you've not changed for the better at all.*

I hovered over post the album and realized I had two choices. Feel the discomfort and grow, knowing I wasn't perfect, that there is no perfect. Or don't post them and stay in a comfort zone—don't change.

Limiting my freedom was not worth it. I hit post. And the world did not end. I had been on vacation, I had gained a few pounds. I had missed a few runs. I had been frustrated and had a spat with Jack over directions to the park. I had promised myself I'd run each day and I hadn't. None of that equaled failure.

I made choices and I was now seeing the result of the choices. The effect. I did not like it. So I channeled Grace once again. My inner-grace: *What do you do Jane? Feel bad and gain more weight? Stay in insolation and feel depressed? Or tune out the negative banter? Ask for help and get on with the happiness habits?*

PART VI
SOUL SHIFT OF COLLATERAL HAPPINESS

Experiencing Collateral Happiness
Side Effects of Transformation
The Fear of Our Own Ego

Experiencing Collateral Happiness

Experiencing collateral happiness may involve a soul-shifting transformation—a shift from living of ego (as part of our identity) to that of living and breathing the authentic self.

Ego serves a vital purpose as part of our human 'life on earth' as a means for survival. **Ego is not our identity. It is not who we are. It is not the spiritual self.** In understanding the Ego's role we can go beyond survival. We can thrive.

Think of Ego as being a function of the mind as a piece of our human consciousness. Ego is similar to that of an instrument, akin to a tool—not a weapon. The diversity among us makes Ego one of the most difficult concepts to understand. Perhaps one of the following will allow you to let go of the confusion of what Ego is:

- Ego is the shield that provides a layer of protection—no self-respecting Knight would go into battle without one.

- Ego is an intruder warning system, alerting us to suspected prowlers—even when, sometimes, they are not prowlers, but innocent dog-walkers.

- Ego is a car alarm—we are compelled to check why it was set off.

- Ego is the yellow light between the green and the red—when we are required to make decisions in a split second based on a flashing light.

- Ego is the lawnmower in the shed—it will cut your lawn to desirable lengths creating a beautiful landscape if operated well, but it has the power to damage and destroy if not used with care and attention.

However you metaphorize Ego, one thing is for sure: we all have the power to purpose our Ego. To learn to recognize and control it as the 'shield' and not the 'power' is an incredible feat which leads to the shift or transformation. To combine that knowledge with the steps of awareness and self-love, is to rise a spiral staircase to a level where we experience all aspects of collateral happiness.

Many people will ask, "How will I know if and when I've had this transformation?"

Everyone wants to know how to recognize success and a final 'membership' into a group of the 'transformed'.

Asking about transformation is like asking: how do you know your partner is *the one*? The thing is, transformation is not like achieving or attaining a medal or trophy. Transformation is a 'state' of experiencing.

Transformation is a 'shift' in the complete self. A 'shift' where one feels and knows transformation has taken place.

Authentic self is of feeling—an innate sense of knowing. Ego is thinking. Transformation is a shift in our complete being where we begin to lead by what we feel and not by what we think—living life based on the internal virtues of authentic self, rather than the external virtues of ego.

Somewhere along our life path, typically childhood, we assume the voice of ego as the primary lead. We begin to lose touch with our authentic self and begin to seek approval by impressing others. **This creates disharmony within our being because authentic self does not exist to impress, only to express.**

Stifling and withholding authentic expression creates imbalance in the body—one can feel trapped inside one's self, as if suffocating—identifying with words such as 'stuck', 'imprisoned', and 'restricted'. There will be a longing, deep within, to 'feel' free.

It is our purpose to learn how to differentiate and allow our authentic self to lead, and yet allow the ego to guide by alerting us to potential danger—danger as we've redefined it as through the steps of collateral happiness.

To recognize where you may be at in your own collateral happiness journey, this list covers the top five pre-transformation (or pre-shift) virtues from women. Note that they are Ego-based external virtues.

1. Family
2. Independence
3. Career
4. Fitting In
5. Attractiveness

However, after a transformation or 'shift' into collateral happiness, responses move to authentic-based virtues:

1. Personal Growth
2. Self-Esteem
3. Spirituality
4. Happiness
5. Forgiveness

Similarly, answers from males in the pre-shift (Ego based) stage echoed:

1. Money
2. Adventure
3. Achievement
4. Pleasure
5. Respect (to be respected)

Post-shift values—authentic-self based living internal virtues were reported as:

1. Spirituality
2. Personal Peace
3. Family
4. God's will/Purpose
5. Honest and Integrity

It bears repeating, there is no right or wrong way to live.
- There is cause and effect.
- Our choices result in a feeling of emptiness or one of fulfillment.
- It is our free will to choose.

Most want to breeze through and say, 'alright, got it'. They want to skip the steps of creating happiness and self-love and jump straight to fulfillment. Many will speak about a 'transformation' in order to convince themselves it happened; others will do the work sporadically and temporarily.

To waiver or wander is to miss the opportunity to feel inner-peace, true-happiness and complete fulfillment.

Reaching true inner-happiness, and obtaining collateral happiness is not about attaining a trophy. Nor is it a destination or checking off boxes in a list. It is the result of habits, beliefs, actions, steps, and feelings constantly and consistently implemented in life-time growth. It is not achieved in a day or weekend retreat. It is not about doing, but about being.

If you are still 'thinking' or 'wondering' whether you have experienced the transformation, then know that you are still being led by Ego.

Remember, the transformation is not something we **think**, but something we **feel, know and experience**.

When we begin to live a life led by authentic self, when challenges appear, we will find ourselves asking the question "what would authentic self need?"

People who are truly authentic don't live in a self-centered world. They also think about, and respect, the authenticity of others. They have good etiquette including sending thank-you notes, acknowledging important life events, being polite and respectful to others, dressing and presenting themselves in a style of their own which also honours the event or occasion (they are considerate of others). They don't need to stand out because they already value their own authenticity and don't need the approval or distinction of others.

> *He who knows much about others may be learned, but he who understands himself is more intelligent. He who controls others may be powerful, but he who has mastered himself is mightier still.*
>
> Lao-Tsu, Tao Teh King

Collateral happiness is an ongoing master-crafting; a life-time of learning, achieving, growing, and appreciating.

Collateral happiness is not a passive program—not one from which we graduate.

No one person is a success story overnight. Growth takes time. Hard work does not always instantly pay off. Rather than struggle and dwell on the lack of reward or achievement, it's better to focus on maximizing our full potential to express authentic self. It is important to practice patience, and put in the work, without the expectation of instant results. There will be a payoff. That is a guarantee. There is, however, no guarantee of when.

Keep pushing. Keep working. Keep focusing. Keep striving. Remember:
Luck is not lucky—it is opportunity meeting preparation.

Side Effects Of Transformation

The closer we get to collateral happiness and your authentic self, the less we are able to tolerate feeling anything less.

- You might edit your circle of friends.
- You may influence others.
- People might leave you.
- People may join you.
- You might no longer be able to tolerate your work conditions.
- You may improve and become a game-changer at your company.
- You might no longer enjoy certain foods.
- You may discover long-forgotten taste buds.
- You might continue to question whether there is something wrong with you.
- You may enjoy glimpsing new, powerful images of yourself.
- You might question why situations don't work out.
- You may delight in clarity and welcome opportunity.
- You might question if you are on the right path.
- You may enjoy the journey regardless of the route.

The farther along we travel on the 'collateral happiness' path, the less we tolerate inauthenticity. Sometimes we lose—people, situations, material objects, goals, dreams, ideals, experiences. Sometimes we gain. The loss or gain is an alignment to how authentic we choose to live.

Rise to Collateral Happiness
There is Great Power Behind Your Facade.

Roar Jane, Roar

"Change is such a bitch," I said to Grace.

Grace laughed. "'Adventure is not outside; it is within.' David Grayson said that."

"Sometimes it's safer to stay inside. Especially when it's dark out," I said.

"'A decision made from fear is always the wrong decision.' Tony Robbins," said Grace. "Have you redone your happiness chart?"

"All 10's in one to five years," I said. "I'm aiming high."

"And... Have you told her yet?" asked Grace.

"I've shown her, but I've not told her," I replied.

"Are you close to telling her?"

"I'm planning a ceremony."

"A ceremony? That's fantastic," said Grace.

"I was hoping you'd be okay with me doing the ceremony here, today. I've always loved that mirror over there."

"Do you want me to leave?" she asked.

"I'd like you to stay. You decide. I won't be hurt either way. I don't know where you are at right now. I only know where I am," I said.

"I want to stay," said Grace.

"Absolutely," I replied.

I'd checked my mascara in that mirror so many times, but this time I could have sworn I was two or three inches taller. Maybe she'd rehung it.

"Wait," said Grace. She grabbed a tissue. "I always cry at ceremonies."

I focused my whole heart and soul on my reflection—more intensely than a fictional Alice might, more curious too. I observed the way my lips prepared for speech. And then I spoke the words I had been waiting my whole life to hear from me.

"I LOVE you."

Notes For Our Growth
On the Fear of Our Own Ego

Twenty years ago, I had no idea that it would take me 'twenty years' to figure out my passion and purpose. At the time, I had hoped it would take a month. That was my continual expectation. So for twenty years, every other month, I would feel like a failure and go into a depressive state because I never fulfilled my expectation. I periodically felt I had no meaning. I lived in an existential vacuum. It was exhausting living in highs and lows, and a drain on me and my family.

During those two decades, I didn't sit idle. I collected information. I got a diploma in finance, and a degree in business. I eventually became a strategy and planning business analyst. I thought this was my purpose. Three years later, I crashed and burned because it didn't work out. I had no back up plan. I thought I'd wasted nine years of my life.

Eventually, I let that go and decided to study Reiki and energy healing. I thought my purpose was to be an energy healer. I was really good at it, but it didn't work out. I continued on and then decided to study nutrition; being a nutritionist didn't work out either. I then studied coaching, to supplement my nutrition skills. Wanna guess the next line? You're right, nutrition coaching didn't work out either. Then I studied Sho Tai, iridology, and Quantum Biofeedback so that I could combine them with coaching, nutrition, and energy. No surprise here, being a wellness practitioner didn't work out. I studied Indian Head Massage so I could combine energy healing with the physical body. And it did not work out.

For more than twenty years I amassed a wealth of knowledge in business and wellness, yet I had nothing to show for it. I felt like the ultimate failure. A twenty-year disappointment in the making.

Collateral Happiness: The Power Behind the Facade

Life felt futile. I couldn't catch my breath. I had all this skill and all this knowledge, and was ready to throw it away to start completely anew. I was depressed and lost. All because I still could not see my purpose. I saw my experience and knowledge as garbage.

Separately none of my skills worked the way I wanted them to, but together they made me a powerhouse. I just hadn't discovered it yet. Nor had I fully learned the mindset to embrace it.

I persisted through my fears and tuned out my ego. I decided I would take one last stab before I called defeat and succumbed to the reliance on a small coloured pill to take away my pain.

I sat down and wrote a book. Each day I vowed to write from my heart space—my authentic self. I chose to never rely on ego or my thinking space. The book started as a diet book, which turned into a memoir, which then turned into a system of happiness.

I had no idea that twenty years of learning, all that effort, had a purpose; each piece a part of a puzzle that was to be assembled to fully understand and see my purpose.

Each discipline and area I'd researched and studied, experienced and experimented with trial and error, had been a gift. Each one a significant piece to be assembled into a more complex, intricate, multi-dimensional living, breathing work of art.

I thought each piece was garbage when, individually, it did not work out. I did not know, during those twenty years, each experience was part of a larger masterpiece: a system to help me and others overcome unhappiness. A system to offer others.

You see, in the process and in my work, I never knew the final outcome. That was my life lesson. To follow a step-by-step process and to learn how to trust and use faith to determine each step in front of me without seeing the summit, or without seeing two steps ahead. I only got to see one step at a time.

Not all of us are blessed to see the summit or the steps in one swooping glance. We think this is our disadvantage; the universe playing games with us, that we are unlucky. But this is not true. Hidden deep within is the greatest gift and lesson of all. It is our purpose to uncover the gift and to assemble piece by piece the ultimate masterpiece.

Don't throw out pieces of a masterpiece before they are all assembled. To do this would be to throw out life's greatest gift—meaning and fulfillment with enduring collateral happiness.

Don't throw out 'invaluable pieces' before you learn what they are for. It is your responsibility to learn how to assemble them. You may need to discover more pieces; have appreciation for each piece. Find friends, experts, strategies, and tools to help you build each part. Enjoy the process of putting together the masterpiece. In time, you will hold happiness and appreciation for the ultimate blessing and gift in its completion.

To be gifted the masterpiece as a whole, in the beginning, rather than the individual pieces, is to not fully appreciate its creation. The true value of the gift is appreciating the significance of each intricate piece. It is one thing to possess something magnificent, but even better to appreciate that magnificence through valuing its every step of construction, knowing you built it piece by piece, and understanding the intricacy of each step.

We can each hold an assembled work of art. The truth and true happiness is in learning, discovering the assembly process, and appreciating its creation. Purposeful life, filled with collateral happiness comes from knowing you grew, learned, and fulfilled your own manifestation and transcendence.

The Afterlogue of the Higher Self

When this labour of love, *Collateral Happiness*, was in its final stages, I became overwhelmed with fear. Will people want to read this book? Should I continue?

Even as a seasoned collateral happiness-er, I regressed. And I owned it. Self-awareness does that, keeps one honest. As does self-love.

I spent two weeks in and out of discomfort. Then I wrote a version of what you see below.

I still have days I struggle, regress, feel depressive and think negatively. I've just learned to recognize the calls to action, turned down the destructive banter and have become a much friendlier companion to myself.

And so it begins...

> Christine your eyes look puffy.
> I will make more time to sleep and rest.
>
> You've spent so much time writing and proofing. Is anyone going to buy your book?
> I can't control that. I gave my absolute best in writing it and learned an abundance of value in the process.
>
> Is there enough value in your book for readers?
> Again, I gave it my all and learned an immeasurable amount.
>
> Your pants are a bit snug.
> I'll get my 80-20 eating back in line. Not a big deal.
>
> Your work is not going as well as you hoped—it's you.
> Yes. It's time to address my weakness, expand my skills, and learn even more.

The Afterlogue of the Higher Self

I am on the right career path.
I really love my husband and kids. I am blessed.
I am in competition with no one.
I am here to be better than I was yesterday.
I'm not here to impress anyone.
I am here to express my power and purpose.
I deserve all the success and happiness in the world.
I have the power to make it happen.
I am proud of myself.
I am learning.
I am so blessed.
I feel stunning.
I love who I am.

I AM HAPPY.

The completion of this book broke the negative pattern, not me. There is nothing wrong with me.

It took me years, but I learned how to retrain, recondition and control my mindset.

I shut down TBSN (The Burden of Shame Network) and tuned into my inner power. Adjusted the volume to high. And I, finally, piece by piece, let my facade fall away.

About the Author

Christine Waldner lives and thrives with her husband and two children in Calgary, Alberta.

Holding a degree in Business, and with more than a decade of research and experience in the subject of wellness, she is a well-known and much appreciated life coach. This is her first book.

Made in the USA
Columbia, SC
15 April 2018